SIX
BLACK MASTERS
OF
AMERICAN ART

The aim of Zenith Books is to present the history and culture of minority groups in the United States and their participation in the growth and development of the country. Through histories, biographies, literature, and the arts, Zenith Books will increase the awareness among all people of minority-group heritage and at the same time develop an understanding and appreciation of that heritage.

ZENITH BOOKS SERIES CONSULTANT: John Hope Franklin

Dr. John Hope Franklin, professor in the History Department at the University of Chicago, has also taught at Brooklyn College, Fisk University, and Howard University. For the year 1962–63 he was Pitt Professor of American History and Institutions at Cambridge University in England. He is the author of many books, including *From Slavery to Freedom, The Militant South, Reconstruction After the Civil War*, and *The Emancipation Proclamation*.

GENERAL EDITOR: Milton Meltzer

Milton Meltzer is the author of many highly successful books for all age groups. His publications include *In Their Own Words: A History of the American Negro; Langston Hughes, a Biography*; and *Thaddeus Stevens and the Fight for Negro Rights*. Mr. Meltzer collaborated with Langston Hughes on *A Pictorial History of the Negro in America* and *Black Magic*.

ROMARE BEARDEN is one of the most prominent Black artists living today. In 1967 he was awarded the annual prize of the National Academy of Arts and Letters. His work has appeared in many museums, including one-man shows at the Corcoran Gallery in Washington, D.C., and at the Museum of Modern Art in New York City. He is co-author of a book, *The Painter's Mind*.

HARRY HENDERSON has contributed many articles to such magazines as *McCall's, Harper's, Redbook, Cosmopolitan*, and the now defunct *Collier's*. Among other things, he reported on the wartime experiences in America of such refugee artists as Marc Chagall, Fernand Léger, Jacques Lipchitz, and André Masson. He has collaborated on the research for this book for many years with Mr. Bearden, a long-time friend.

SIX
BLACK MASTERS
OF
AMERICAN ART

ROMARE BEARDEN
and
HARRY HENDERSON

ZENITH BOOKS
DOUBLEDAY & COMPANY, INC., GARDEN CITY
NEW YORK

The Zenith Books edition, published simultaneously in hardbound and paperback volumes, is the first publication of *Six Black Masters of American Art.*

ISBN: 0-385-01211-X TRADE
0-385-01537-2 PREBOUND

Zenith Books Edition: 1972
Library of Congress Catalog Card Number 70–175358
Copyright © 1972 by Romare Bearden and Harry Henderson
All Rights Reserved
Printed in the United States of America
9 8 7 6 5 4 3 2

Cover Credits: Joshua Johnston's *Unknown Cleric* (Bowdoin College Museum of Art, Brunswick, Me.); Robert S. Duncanson's *Blue Hole, Flood Waters, Little Miami River* (Cincinnati Museum of Art); Henry Ossawa Tanner's *Return from the Cross* (Merton D. Simpson, New York City); Horace Pippin's *Roses with Red Chair* (David H. H. Felix, Philadelphia); Augusta Savage's *Gamin* (Schomburg Collection, New York Public Library); Jacob Lawrence's *In the North the Negro had better educational facilities* from the series *The Migration of the Negro* (Museum of Modern Art, New York City).

ACKNOWLEDGMENTS

We are indebted to more individuals and institutions for assistance in preparing these sketches of the lives of six American artists of African descent than we can name in this short space. We are particularly indebted to Robert Luck and Jemison Hammond, Archives of American Art, New York City; Violette de Mazia, Barnes Foundation, Merion, Pa.; Robert Carlen, Carlen Gallery, Philadelphia; Francis W. Robinson, Detroit Institute of Art; Luise Ross, Terry Dintenfass Gallery, New York City; Warren M. Robbins, Frederick Douglass Institute, Washington, D.C.; David Driskell, Fisk University, Nashville, Tenn.; Helen Sanger, Frick Art Reference Library, New York City; Erwin S. Barrie, Grand Central Art Galleries, New York City; John Simon Guggenheim Foundation, New York City; Mary Beatty Brady, Harmon Foundation, New York City; Abram Lerner and Francis R. Shapiro, Joseph H. Hirshhorn Collection, New York City; the late James A. Porter and his wife, Mrs. Dorothy B. Porter, Howard University, Washington, D.C.; M. Lalance, Meudon-la-Forêt, France; Carleton Thorp, Peter A. Juley & Son, New York City; Milton Kaplan, Library of Congress, Washington, D.C.; James D. Parks, Lincoln University, Jefferson City, Mo.; Eugenia Calvert Holland, Maryland Historical Society, Baltimore; Edward H. Dwight, Munson-Williams-Proctor Institute, Utica, N.Y.; Antionette Hure, Ministère des Affaires Culturelles, Musée National d'art Moderne, Paris, France; Patricia Jobling and Richard L. Tooke, Museum of Modern Art, New York City; Roswell P. Russell, Baltimore, Md.; United States National Archives and Records, Washington, D.C.; John Walker, National Gallery of Art, Washington, D.C.; Jean Blackwell Hutson, Schomburg Collection, New York Public Library; National Collection of Fine Arts, Smithsonian Institution, Washington, D.C.; Jesse O. Tanner, Le Douhet, France; Donald Gallup, Yale University Library; Jay Leyda, Yale University, New Haven, Conn.

Charles Alston, Elton Fax, Palmer Hayden, Jacob Lawrence, Hale Woodruff, and numerous other artists furnished data, recollections, and other materials. Joseph P. Henderson assisted in research and photography and Annette Rohan in preparation of the manuscript.

Owners of various works not only granted permission to reproduce them but assisted in other ways. For all their time and care, we thank them.

Romare Bearden
Harry Henderson

CONTENTS

CONTENTS

JOSHUA JOHNSTON
(17___–18___)

National Gallery of Art. Gift of Edgar William and Bernice Chrysler
Garbisch

Johnston's portrait of the Westwood children, members of a
leading Maryland family, shows how painters of that day often
put animals in paintings of children to increase interest.

"Now pull it tight," Joshua Johnston told his young son
who drew a piece of canvas taut over a light wooden
frame while his father quickly tacked it down. "That's
fine! Now let's do the other side."

That spring in 1805, Joshua was planning a painting

trip that would take him into Harford County, north of
Baltimore. "I want to go places where other painters
haven't been. That way I can do more likenesses," he had
told his wife. Yet he did not relish the idea of going into
plantation country, where he might be challenged to prove
he was a free Black man. Mustn't forget to take my
freedom papers, he thought.

Around the room in which he and his son worked
were blank canvases and some portraits without faces.
Among these there were stout figures of men in white
ruffled collars and black coats, slender men with silver
buttons on their jackets. There were faceless ladies in
gowns, seated in large chairs. There were faceless little
girls by garden gates and young boys beside pillars.

In many portraits of children Joshua had painted a
playful little dog, cat, or squirrel because these animals
amused people and helped to sell the painting.

These faceless portraits were very much like cutout
paintings in amusement park photo shops today, in which
a person sticks his head into a hole in the painting from
the rear and is then photographed—riding a bucking bronco,
flying a rocket, or wearing a funny old-fashioned bathing
suit. The painter could let his customer select "the figure"
he wanted. Then the face could be painted in, usually in
one sitting. This saved time for everyone. It also provided
plain farmers and village storekeepers with finer looking
clothes than they actually owned. Because of the way they
worked, such portrait painters were often called "face-
painters," or limners. Joshua Johnston, like most artists
in the period following the Revolution, did some face-
painting, but he was also capable of making true portraits
of people as they sat for him.

As he was loading his canvases into a borrowed wagon,
Joshua got word that the McCormick family wanted him

to paint likenesses of the entire family of five. "Did you hear that?" Joshua cried to his wife. "Five likenesses at one time! That's more work than a trip would provide."

"Don't count your eggs yet, Joshua," cautioned his wife. She had seen times when people changed their minds, times when the only painting Joshua could get to do was varnishing the captain's quarters on ships and making signs for shops and taverns.

That afternoon Joshua Johnston, dressed in his best broadcloth coat and carrying a portfolio and some brushes, presented himself at the fine residence of James McCormick, a leading merchant of Baltimore.

Having been in elegant homes before, he was not surprised at the fine furniture, stately rooms, and glimmering chandeliers. He was ushered into the presence of Mrs. McCormick, who smiled. "I have seen some likenesses that you have painted and I liked them," she said.

"Thank you," said Joshua, naturally pleased.

"I want us all in one painting—my husband, the three children, and myself. Could you do that?"

Joshua hesitated. "That's larger than most paintings I do," he said. "Naturally, Mrs. McCormick, it costs more."

"Don't worry about the cost. My husband has agreed to it," she assured him.

"Very well, Mrs. McCormick," said Joshua, adding, "I need to look around a bit if you don't mind. And I need to see the children too. I need to arrange you."

"But my husband isn't here," Mrs. McCormick reminded him.

"I know," said Joshua Johnston laughing. "In my mind I have a place for him. Let me make a sketch." Quickly he sketched the group several times. On looking at his last sketch, Mrs. McCormick said she liked it and asked him to discuss it after supper that night with her husband.

That evening Joshua met briefly with Mr. and Mrs. McCormick. They agreed to the arrangement presented in the sketch. "And if you achieve a good likeness, I shall gladly pay what you ask. It's likenesses I want, not a grand painting of skies," said Mr. McCormick.

Next day, Joshua stretched a large canvas and went to the paint shop to purchase some colors. Colors came in powder form, not in tubes, in those days. At home, Joshua ground them into a still finer powder with a druggist's mortar and pestle. Then he could mix the powder with linseed oil and small amounts of varnish as needed. The following day, working from the sketch, he roughly outlined the curves of the sofa on his canvas; he especially liked the sofa, which Mrs. McCormick had told him was a Sheraton that had been made in England.

Setting up his canvas in the McCormick home, Joshua began painting, starting with the children. Then he portrayed Mrs. McCormick and outlined the figure of Mr. McCormick. He next filled in the background of the painting and one morning when Mr. McCormick did not go to his office in order to pose for him, Joshua completed his portrait of the family. The McCormicks were delighted with it. Joshua listened to their praise with satisfaction.

Shortly after that, the McCormicks had a party at which their friends and relatives had a chance to see the new family portrait. It won much praise. Although Joshua Johnston had been painting some of the most socially important people in Baltimore for nearly ten years, it was still a surprise to many of them to find that a Black man could paint so well. Joshua portrayed his sitters in a direct and straightforward manner. At times his painting seemed a little stiff, but he caught his sitters' self-confidence and pride in their achievements in a charming way. His portraits of children were rendered with a de-

Collections of the Maryland Historical Society

Joshua Johnston's portrait of the family of wealthy Baltimore merchant James McCormick shows that he was a master of composition. Johnston liked to paint his subjects seated on furniture with brass-tacked upholstery.

lightful innocence. After the McCormick family portrait, he had many more orders.

There were, of course, Black men who drew and painted in America before Joshua Johnston. Many were artisans, engravers, and goldsmiths. Gilbert Stuart, reproductions of whose portraits of George Washington are in virtually every school, "derived his first impression of drawing from witnessing Neptune Thurston, a slave who was employed on his master's cooper-shop, sketch likenesses on the heads of casks," according to Edward Peterson's 1853 *History of Rhode Island.* The following newspaper advertisement from the Boston *News-Letter,* January 7, 1773, indicates the existence of still another Black artist:

family, the legend said that the painter was a Negro blacksmith, the slave of General John Stricker, who had also distinguished himself in the War of 1812. In the third family the legend was that the painter had been a slave of Colonel John Moale (1731–98), who led the Baltimore militia during the Revolution, and afterwards became the Presiding Judge of Baltimore County Court and a leading merchant, landowner, and political leader in the state government. In the Moale family the legend was that the slave was called William Johnson and that, in his later years, he was cared for by one of the subjects whom he painted—Mrs. John Moale. The Moale descendants also say he was the slave of a "well-known artist whose name cannot now be recalled," to quote Dr. Pleasants. In a fourth family the legend claimed that the artist had come from the West Indies to Baltimore, but his name and race and whether or not he was a slave were not part of the legend.

Examining the paintings of these families by these legendary Black painters, Dr. Pleasants found some remarkable similarities in style and method of painting. Like other art experts, Dr. Pleasants considered the artist's true signature to be the *way* he actually paints—how the hands are painted, the face, the costume, the pose, the eyes and mouth, the use of various props such as books or baskets or furniture and how they are painted.

But if the same artist had painted them, which of the legends was true? Dr. Pleasants found he could not make himself believe that this same artist had been a slave who was sold from one family to the next or that he was "hired out" by his master to paint portraits.

He then began a systematic search of the old city directories. He soon found a "Joshua Johnston" listed as a portrait painter from 1796 to 1824. The name "William

Johnson," given by the Moale descendants, perhaps
prompted Dr. Pleasants to examine this name with care.
Sometimes he found Joshua Johnston's name spelled without the "t."

When he got to the directory for 1817, one in which
free Black men were listed separately as "Free Householders
of Colour," he found Joshua Johnston listed in that section as a portrait painter living on Nelson Street in the
old section of Baltimore. Slaves were never listed, and in
other years the names of free Black householders were
designated as "(black man)" or with an asterisk (*).

Dr. Pleasants then searched the 1810 census. He found
Joshua Johnston listed, without a street address, with
his wife, three boys under fifteen years old and two girls
under ten, and another adult, possibly his mother or
mother-in-law. He was not listed in the 1820 census,
perhaps because he was painting out of Baltimore.

Joshua Johnston moved frequently and lived in many
places. In 1800 he lived in Baltimore on Primrose Alley,
from 1802 to 1804 at North Gay Street. Then his name
disappeared from the city directory. Through his portraits
Dr. Pleasants traced him to Cecil and Harford counties
north of Baltimore. In 1814, back in the city, he lived
on Strawberry Alley, and in 1817, as already noted, on
Nelson Street. In 1819 he had moved to the newer part
of the city, to St. Paul's Lane, near Centre Street, and in
1824 he had moved back to the old town.

While tracing all these movements on old maps, Dr.
Pleasants found that in 1796 Joshua Johnston was on
German Street between Hanover and Howard streets.
Colonel John Moale then had a townhouse and garden
there and "possibly Johnston was given painting room
space in a small building on the Moale property," noted
Dr. Pleasants.

Johnston's name disappeared from the city directories in 1824. This probably was because he was painting in the outlying counties or on the eastern shore of Maryland. The latest painting for which Dr. Pleasants could establish a date was 1832, when Joshua Johnston painted the children of Clement Cox, a prominent citizen of the eastern shore area.

Of the possibility that perhaps the painter had come from the West Indies, Dr. Pleasants found little evidence. Between 1793 and 1795 more than 1,000 French refugees fled to Baltimore from Haiti to escape the successful revolution against slavery of the Black people led by Toussaint L'Ouverture. Many of the refugees brought with them slaves that they considered loyal to them.

But so great was the fear of slave revolts in the United States that these slaves were viewed with suspicion. Many states refused to admit them.

All this makes it most unlikely that at that time so many prominent Baltimore and Maryland families would accept in their midst a French-speaking Black painter. And had Joshua Johnston been a white artist from the French West Indies, he must have changed his name to Joshua Johnston, for it is not French. There were white French artists and silversmiths who came to Maryland from Haiti but they proudly retained their French names. The indications thus are that Joshua Johnston, whether born slave or free, was a native Black American.

In his study of Johnston's painting, Dr. Pleasants noted the rigid way in which the arms and hands are painted and that, with few exceptions, the face is presented in a three-quarter view. The eyes and mouth are strikingly the same in all portraits, with the sitters apparently staring at the painter. The children are nearly always posed in the same way, with expressionless hands, but in his later work these portraits became more charming and personal. In nineteen of a group of twenty-one paintings, the hands hold objects like letters, charts, books, baskets, whistles, fruit, or cake. In paintings with baskets of strawberries and cherries the basket-weave is identical. The Sheraton sofa, studded with brass tacks in the McCormick family portrait, is repeated in other paintings; in some, chairs are shown with brass tacks. Usually the fruit and costumes are painted with great care.

How and where Joshua Johnston learned to paint is still a mystery. He may have been a house or ship painter at first. Seeking to identify Johnston's teacher, Dr. Pleasants compared his work with that of other artists in the area at the time. He was quickly able to establish certain similarities between Johnston's work and that of Charles Peale Polk, who was a portrait painter in Baltimore. Polk had learned to paint from his uncle, Charles Willson Peale, along with Peale's sons, Raphael, Rembrandt, Rubens, and Titian. Rembrandt Peale also settled in Baltimore for a while as a portrait painter; he used to advertise "No likeness, no pay."

Johnston's work most closely resembled Polk's work in its somewhat stiff figures. Johnston also used some of the same devices—the red draperies, books, and pillars that Polk was fond of using. Both Johnston and Polk applied their paint sparingly. But while Polk used brighter and more varied colors, Johnston's colors were restrained, painted in strong, almost black-and-white contrast. He favored somber backgrounds and costumes. As he matured, he relied more on areas of purer, brighter color than his quiet palette—that is, his range of color—of earlier years.

Two additional circumstantial facts have been uncovered by the authors of the present book. One is that Charles Willson Peale was an abolitionist and might well have encouraged his nephew Polk to teach a Black man. He helped one of his own slaves, whom he set free, to earn a comfortable living making silhouettes at his famous museum in Philadelphia.

The second fact relates to the possibility that Joshua Johnston may have originally been a slave of Colonel John Moale who was an amateur artist himself as a young man. He made portraits and landscapes of early Baltimore and owned paintings and engravings. Conceivably he could have encouraged Joshua Johnston as an artist, perhaps provided him with a few lessons, and given or let him earn his freedom.

But if he ever was a slave, exactly how Joshua Johnston became a free Black man is not known with certainty.

What is not a mystery is life in fast-growing Baltimore in those days. In 1790, when Joshua Johnston was presumably getting started, the city had 13,503 people. Ten years later the population had doubled. By 1810 there were 46,000 people there—36,192 whites, 5,671 free Blacks, and 4,672 slaves. The number of free Black people greatly alarmed the city's slaveholders because, among other things, they voted. The slaveholders succeeded in getting a law passed forbidding this—and another forbidding the settling in Baltimore of more free Blacks.

What drew free Black men to Baltimore was the chance of learning a trade in this rapidly growing city, with its booming shipyards and brickyards. Its shipyards created the American clipper, the fastest sailing ship on the seas.

Among the Black people of the city were some outstanding men. The best known of them was Benjamin Banneker, a genius who impressed scholars of his time with his mechanical and mathematical abilities. His protests against slavery to Thomas Jefferson and his demonstrated mathematical ability led to his being made a member of the commission that laid out Washington, D.C. Banneker's Almanac carried his portrait in a wood engraving that may have been based on a painting by Joshua Johnston.

Another eminent Black leader of Baltimore at that time was the Reverend Daniel Coker, a founder of the African Methodist Episcopal Church. He wrote and published anti-slavery pamphlets in 1812. A painting of a Black clergyman by Joshua Johnston exists in the Bowdoin College Museum of Art. Whether or not this is a portrait of Rev. Coker is unknown. But doubtless Joshua Johnston knew Rev. Coker, who had organized "Sabbath schools" in Baltimore that taught reading, writing, and arithmetic to Black children. The schools Rev. Coker organized even attracted children from Washington.

Joshua Johnston apparently had the opportunity to acquire a broader education than was possible for most Black people in the South at the time. He was probably a pleasant conversationalist, able to chat amiably with his subjects and to get them to relax while they posed for him. This could have been a delicate problem for anyone who was not self-assured and confident of his success. His adult sitters were slaveowners who, as a rule, feared free Black men. That Joshua Johnston painted so many leading Baltimoreans would indicate that his work was highly regarded and that he was personable. Unlike Rembrandt Peale, who used the city newspapers to advertise himself as a portrait painter, there is no record of advertisements by Johnston—although perhaps newspapers refused his advertisements. Thus his reputation apparently grew by word of mouth and the endorsement of his sitters.

Yet Baltimore laws would require Joshua Johnston to carry "freedom papers," giving his height and weight, signed by either his former owner or an eminent man, attesting to the fact that he was free and of good character. Baltimore, as already noted, was a major slave-trading center, with large sheds on the waterfront for holding slaves for auction to planters from Georgia, Mississippi, and Alabama. In view of these circumstances, it is almost certain that Joshua Johnston could not have had continuous access to the city's leading families unless a prominent Baltimorean had vouched for him. Either Colonel Moale, General Stricker, or General Smith would qualify, and if one of them were in fact his former owner, Johnston's access to these families might be explained.

When, on June 18, 1812, the United States declared war on England, Joshua Johnston was inevitably thrown into the very center of the question gripping both white and Black Baltimoreans. The merchants and shipowners of the city were divided about the war. Of prime concern to Joshua Johnston would be the fact that the British fleet, marauding along Chesapeake Bay, was offering freedom to slaves who joined them. And many slaves did just that. Free Black men in Baltimore, who outnumbered the slaves in the city, discussed the course they should take. Could they oppose a slave's seeking freedom? Could they, by fighting loyally for the United States, win freedom for their Black brothers and sisters? What did the British offer the free Black man? The issue hardened when, in the spring of 1813, British marines, accompanied by newly freed and armed Black men, landed at Havre de Grace and burned it. Joshua Johnston, with personal acquaintanceships among the leading circles of Baltimore, was in an unusual position for a black man, for he could witness the panic this news touched off among slaveholders.

The British fleet easily blockaded Chesapeake Bay's only outlet to the sea—the narrow opening, between Cape

Henry and Cape Charles. This brought Baltimore to a standstill. Cargoes rotted on the dockyards and most shipyard workers and laborers were unemployed. Many of those who lost their jobs were free Black men.

Among Black people, discussions were held continuously about which course they should take. Rev. Coker, Joshua Johnston, and other well-informed Black men probably participated in these quiet dialogues daily. From Philadelphia came word that the Reverend Richard Allen and the Reverend Absalom Jones, founders of the African Methodist Episcopal Church, were leading their congregations in building fortifications there.

The British offer of freedom was attractive to those held in bondage. What reduced its appeal was the notorious record of the British as slave traders. How could Black people be sure they would not be sold in the Caribbean if they went over to the British?

The majority of the free Black men and women of Baltimore concluded that they should fight in defense of their homes, families, and liberty. However harsh their lot, they had already escaped the yoke of slavery and they felt that by fighting loyally for the United States they could win respect and freedom for their Black brothers and sisters in bondage. Indeed, some had won their freedom by fighting in the American Revolution. Nevertheless, some of those held in slavery seized this opportunity to end their oppression and slipped away.

With the British controlling Chesapeake Bay, Baltimore's leaders concluded that they might be attacked any day. They organized a Committee on Vigilance and Safety, which called a town meeting to prepare the defense of Baltimore. Joshua Johnston may have attended this meeting which called upon all classes of people for help. On the morning of August 28, 1813, defense assignments were posted for all those not in uniform: "with spades, wheelbarrows, pick axes and shovels—the exempts from military service and free people of color of the first district . . . assemble tomorrow, Sunday morning, at 6 o'clock at Hampstead Hill with provisions for the day. . . ."

This was to be the major defense line of the city and it can be presumed that Joshua Johnston helped dig places for the hundred cannon dragged there. If he had not participated in the city's defense, one can be certain that he would not have later obtained commissions from eminent military and political leaders such as General Smith and General Stricker.

Yet the expected British attack did not immediately materialize. It was almost a year later when the British fleet, with some 6,000 veterans of Wellington's army, sailed into the Chesapeake. On August 19, 1814, the British disembarked at the mouth of the Patuxent River and marched on Washington. The capital's defenses collapsed, partially because slaveholders, supposed to lead the defense forces, wouldn't leave their plantations lest their slaves flee to the British. The United States military leaders had poorly prepared the defense of Washington. President James Madison was forced to flee the capital, the first and only time this has ever happened to an American President. On August 24 and 25, advancing British troops burned the Capitol, the White House, all but one of the government buildings, and many private residences.

All Baltimore people saw the glow in the sky of burning Washington, only thirty-eight miles away. But they prepared to fight. The British General Ross announced he would make Baltimore his winter quarters. He was contemptuous of its defenses. He would go where he pleased in Maryland, he said. The city's Committee of Vigilance and Safety called for renewal of the city's defenses. The people of Baltimore, "of all classes and conditions," prepared to defend themselves.

On September 11 the British fleet began landing some 6,000 troops at North Point, just outside Baltimore. General Smith and General Stricker, having anticipated their arrival there, let the British advance confidently for several miles. A ragged line of American riflemen kept falling back before them. After the British had moved inland several miles, a Baltimore sharpshooter killed General Ross himself. Then suddenly the British were confronted with the main Baltimore force, some 4,000 men equipped with artillery and cavalry. The British veterans were stopped, pounded back—and they then attempted to pull back during the night. At dawn they found themselves hard pressed, pursued, assaulted by cavalry. The British fleet sent boats to begin to take them off the shore on which they had landed so confidently. They were in grave danger of being wiped out before they could reembark.

That night, September 13, to create a diversion, the British attempted a landing on the city waterfront under cover of a furious bombardment of Fort McHenry in the harbor. All night cannon balls thudded into the fort while Baltimoreans—perhaps including Joshua Johnston— followed the fight anxiously. A watching young lawyer relieved his anxiety by writing "in the dawn's early light" some verses on the back of an old letter addressed to him, Francis Scott Key. The British bombardment failed and Key's verses later became famous as *The Star-Spangled Banner.* They were immediately printed on leaflets in Baltimore, and Joshua Johnston may very well have carried copies home to his family.

When the War of 1812 ended there was a greater demand for portraits than ever, particularly of the city's defenders. For the next ten years Joshua Johnston was kept very busy.

But after 1824 the city directory no longer listed him— and after 1832, when he was painting on the Maryland eastern shore, all trace of him disappears. The Moale family legend, as reported by Roswell P. Russell, the owner of the portrait of Mrs. John Moale and her granddaughter Ellin North Moale, is that Joshua Johnston became ill with consumption; today this would be called emphysema or tuberculosis.

When Mrs. Moale, the widow of Colonel Moale, learned of Johnston's condition, she had him taken to the Moale country estate, Green Spring, about ten miles north of Baltimore. There in the rolling hills he gradually recovered.

To show his gratitude, Joshua Johnston painted a portrait of Mrs. Moale and her granddaughter. Mrs. Moale, well-known as an independent spirit, had already had her portrait painted by six different artists. But this portrait by Joshua Johnston always had a special meaning for her and remained in the family. At one time some members of the family attributed the painting to Charles Willson Peale.

This painting was, according to the Moale family legend, Johnston's last, and he died soon after. However, Dr. Pleasants believed the portrait was completed about 1801 because the child in the painting died in 1803. This was nearly thirty years before the children of Clement Cox were painted by Joshua Johnston. Thus the mystery of Joshua Johnston continues.

Perhaps some day old letters or diaries will clear up the mystery. Ever since Dr. Pleasants first reported the existence of Joshua Johnston the main outlines and features of his life have been gradually emerging. One painting identified as his, the portrait of the McCormick family, was shown in Pittsburgh's Carnegie Institute Museum of Fine Art in 1940. When it was reproduced in *Life*, December 9, 1940, it was recognized by an Illinois woman with a Baltimore background to be the same kind of painting she had of her ancestors, the Kennedy Long family. Her painting was immediately verified as one of Johnston's by Dr. Pleasants. By the time he died, Dr. Pleasants had identified fifty such portraits. Since then others have been identified. Still others will be found and some day perhaps the missing parts of the story of Joshua Johnston will come to light.

In his lifetime Joshua Johnston's work was not exhibited anywhere except in the homes of his sitters. Today his paintings are in the National Gallery of Art in Washington, D.C., the Maryland Historical Society, the Baltimore Museum of Art, and in private collections. Yet most of his portraits remain as the prized possessions of the descendants of people whom he painted nearly two hundred years ago.

According to a Moale family legend told by the present owner, this portrait of Mrs. John Moale and her granddaughter was made out of gratitude by Johnston after Mrs. Moale found him ill and sent him to her estate to recover his health.

Roswell P. Russell, Baltimore, and Frick Art Reference Library

ROBERT S. DUNCANSON
(1822–1872)

Collection of Richard S. Rust III, Cincinnati; photo by Edward H. Dwight

The Caves, painted in 1869, is a fine example of Duncanson's work. Duncanson's painting later became more impressionistic.

"Out of the frying pan, into the fire! That's you!" said many of Robert S. Duncanson's friends in 1841 when he decided to leave the safety of Canada to try to become an artist in Cincinnati, Ohio. Nearly 50,000 Black people from the United States had by then found refuge in Canada. Young Robert, a spirited nineteen-year-old, knew he was traveling the route of the Underground Railroad in reverse. Cincinnati was on the South's border and proslavery in attitude. But it was on the free soil of Ohio and therefore an outpost of freedom for escaping slaves. They headed for it by the hundreds. For years its free Black people and a handful of abolitionists had manned that outpost, hiding runaway slaves until they could be moved northward, in spite of attacks on their homes.

Young Robert knew this. "But I have to go back," he told himself. "I can never develop as an artist where I am isolated from other artists." But why Cincinnati? Why this proslavery city that the average man called "Porkopolis" because its meat packers slaughtered 500,000 pigs for pork each year? Why not Boston? New York? Why go to a city on the physical edge of slavery, plagued with vicious slave hunters—liable to grab any Black man?

For one thing, Robert's mother lived on its outskirts in a village that was abolitionist in its views and had barrel-making and furniture factories. He could live with his mother and get work there, a kind of security he would not have elsewhere. Still more important to young Robert was the fact that Cincinnati had nearly a hundred active artists. Indeed, at the time it was one of the liveliest art centers in America, especially for beginners. And he knew that its artists were, like himself, largely self-taught, from humble origins, and democratic. In the tradition of great artists, they rejected racial prejudice. They were proud that a former Cincinnati hotel lobby-sweeper and clockmaker's assistant, Hiram Powers, had already won world acclaim for his sculpture.

Thus, in the summer of 1841, he left Canada for Mount Pleasant (now Mount Healthy), a village fifteen miles north of Cincinnati, where his mother lived. A well-educated young man, Duncanson had been born in either 1817 or 1822 in upstate New York. His father, a Canadian of Scotch descent, was working there at the time. Apparently because of hostility toward their inter-racial marriage, the Duncansons moved to Cincinnati where Mrs. Duncanson had relatives.

The Duncansons soon found that the large colony of free Black men and abolitionists in Cincinnati ready to help escaping slaves worried Southern slaveholders. The Southerners pressured Cincinnati businessmen, who sold them much equipment and goods, to enforce the old 1807 "Black laws." Under these laws it was a crime to teach a Black man a trade. Black people were denied the right to vote, to bear witness, or serve on juries. A particularly cruel law required every Black person entering Ohio to furnish a $500 bond as a guarantee of good behavior. He also had to furnish a court certificate as evidence of his free status. Without such a certificate he could be considered a runaway slave. This was aimed directly at forcing the free Black people out of Cincinnati. Nearly all of them had originally fled from slavery to Ohio's free soil.

The sudden revival of these laws in 1829 was a signal for proslavery ruffians to attack Black homes in Cincinnati. Leaders of the Black community obtained a sixty-day stay of the "Black laws" while a delegation hurried to Canada to learn if they would be welcome there. Meanwhile, nightly attacks on Black people forced many to flee to Walnut Hills and Mount Pleasant, to northern Ohio.

In Canada the Black delegation was told by Sir James Colebrook, Royal Governor of Upper Canada: "We Royalists do not know men by their color. Should you come to us, you will be entitled to all the privileges of the rest of His Majesty's subjects."

Almost immediately nearly 1,500 Black men, women and children set off for Canada. There they founded Wilberforce, near London, Ontario. Although no documentary evidence exists, it is believed that Duncanson's father, proud of his Canadian heritage, insisted on going and taking young Robert. He felt his son would never get an education in Cincinnati. However, Mrs. Duncanson apparently felt it was best that she stay in Mount Pleasant. Thus young Robert was educated in Canada.

Twelve years passed before he returned. "I've come back to become an artist," he told his mother when she welcomed him at her cottage. He was able to get work in a small furniture factory as a varnisher. He soon realized that Mount Pleasant was a stronghold of abolitionists. Some helped him in his efforts to become an artist.

One September night in 1841, a neighbor leading a half-dozen Black mothers and children, roused the Duncansons. "Brother, we've got to find places for these folks to rest," said the neighbor to Robert. "There's terrible trouble in Cincinnati."

Helping these worn-out refugees into their home, young Robert and his mother listened with anger to the story: A white mob organized in Kentucky was attacking the homes of Black families—just as before in 1829. Black men were being arrested everywhere. Women and children were fleeing. Many Black men were fighting bravely against overwhelming odds in defense of their homes.

The attacks went on for days. The proslavery mob fired a cannon into the Black neighborhood. Finally, to stop the attacks, the Black men agreed to lay down their arms and march to jail. The white mob was supposed to disperse, its leaders having argued they only wanted protection from armed Blacks. But once the Black men were in jail, the mob raced forth to destroy their homes and attack their women and children. They again destroyed the printing presses of the abolitionist paper edited by James G. Birney. "Think, for one moment," said the Cincinnati *Gazette* in a scathing editorial, "of a band calling themselves men disarming, carrying away and securing in prison, the male negroes, promising security and protection to their women and children—and while they were confidently reposing in that security, returning with hellish shouts, to attack these helpless and unprotected persons!"

When word of this reached Mount Pleasant, a solemn Black mother raised her head. "I can't do anything here," she said. "I have to go back to my home in Cincinnati." One by one, others came to the same conclusion. Nobody talked of going to Canada. They were prepared to fight.

Robert and his mother helped these Black mothers and children into wagons to return to the city. There they assembled at the Baker Street Baptist Church to find their families. Some fathers were waiting, but others were dead, missing, or wounded.

John Mercer Langston, later a congressman and an outstanding Black leader, was a boy in Cincinnati at the time. In his autobiography years later he recalled the terror he felt as he ran through the streets to warn his brother and saw Black leaders being forced to hide: "Those were dark days. And they who still survive them may never forget the circumstances of their occurrence, and the public sentiment which, no longer prevalent, made them possible at that time!" These 1841 riots helped Robert Duncanson understand why his father had insisted on taking him to Canada.

At the time he felt sick with anger and anxiety. His idea of becoming an artist there seemed preposterous. He hated and feared the city. Could he be an artist there?

When at last he began to visit white artists in their studios, he was surprised to find himself welcomed. The artists were ashamed of the attacks on Black people and said so. Many had started out just as he was doing—varnishing furniture, painting houses, working at jobs that had given them a chance to feel the action of the brush. Intrigued to find a Black man attempting to become an artist, they took him along on sketching tours. "No better way to learn than to see someone do it," they told him.

Thus Robert Duncanson arrived at the right time to participate in the creation of a type of landscape that impressed Europeans. American art and writing had long been considered second rate. Europe, it seemed, had the great masters in every field and America had nothing important to offer. But in 1841 what was distinctively American was only beginning to emerge—and American landscape painting helped to lead the way.

Back in 1821, shortly before Duncanson was born, a young artist, Thomas Cole, had begun painting landscapes in the Ohio Valley north of Cincinnati. In 1825 he shifted to the Hudson River Valley and the nearby Catskill Mountains in New York. There he created a certain style soon called the "Hudson River School of Painting." Afterward, one who painted in that style was termed an artist of the "Hudson River School."

Cole's work showed what Americans saw when they looked out at their great forests, vast plains, and majestic mountains. In contrast, European landscapes showed cultivated fields and ancient castles or ruins. William Cullen Bryant, an American poet close to nature, pointed out that these paintings of vast wilderness suggested "a power beyond the range of man's ability" and close "to the great mystery of the origin of things."

One factor that made the Hudson River School painters in Cincinnati unique was that they were actually living on the edge of the American wilderness. In those days

Cincinnati was "the West." On sketching tours, camping, and walking, its artists were often true pioneers—the first non-Indians to see steep mountainsides, outstretched plains, the deep gorges carved through rock by swift rivers, the astonishing panoramas seen from peaks.

Coming on these vast, undisturbed scenes, Duncanson, William L. Sonntag, Worthington Whittredge, James Henry Beard, Thomas Buchanan Read, and other Cincinnati artists were filled with excitement. They felt close to God's handiwork. They were proud to be pioneers in showing America's great beauty. And, prophetically, they knew that unpolluted, unravished America was about to disappear before their eyes. They hastened to preserve it in their paintings.

In the beginning, Duncanson had many technical problems to master. No matter how poor he considered his first results, his artist friends encouraged him. He copied popular engravings. He also sketched and painted many scenes around Mount Pleasant—the distant hills, oxcarts on the road, the swamps at the mouth of the Little Miami River which was a major escape route for fugitive slaves.

Leading Cincinnati artists exhibited their work at the Western Art Union. It matched the best gallery in New York in size. A part of its annual show of local artists' work was a lottery for a work by a well-known artist. People as far away as Boston joined the Union in the hope of winning a painting.

Would the Art Union accept the paintings of a Black man? In Cincinnati no Black man dared to go into a theater or restaurant.

"Submit your work," Duncanson's artist friends told him. "You're a local artist. We'll back you up."

He did—and had three paintings accepted for the show of 1842. The city's social leaders turned out to see it.

They took pride in local artists. They wanted the "Queen City of the West" to equal Philadelphia or New York in culture.

But for all its ambitions, Cincinnati was still a Southern city and proslavery in its attitudes. Duncanson told his mother that his delight in having his paintings shown was nearly destroyed by the fact that no one in his family, being Black, could see the exhibit.

"I know," she said. "I'd like to see them there myself. But this is a Southern town. It isn't that I haven't seen the paintings. I know what they look like, and I can stand not seeing them there because I *know they are there!* That's the important thing. They are there!"

Cincinnati abolitionists posted themselves near Duncanson's work. They pointed out that it had been done by a Black man. Some people stormed away in a disbelieving huff. Others praised the work and permitted themselves to be introduced to Duncanson. Although older and better painters won the prizes, Duncanson's work was "what was new" and was much talked about.

Now Duncanson was glad he had come to Cincinnati. He was stimulated by the historical paintings he saw in the exhibit. "I'd like to try that kind of painting," he told his mother. Well-versed in the history of English authors from his Canadian schooling, he decided to copy an engraving of an 1837 painting by Sir George Harvey, a Scottish artist, showing William Shakespeare on trial before Sir Thomas Lucy for poaching. As a young man, according to tradition, Shakespeare had been caught stealing deer and rabbit on Sir Thomas' estate and had been brought before him for punishment. Under English law of that time, a poacher could be sentenced to death. Shakespeare then fled to escape this cruel system.

Duncanson's artist friends complained about his proposed subject. "The scene isn't dramatic enough. Why not Hamlet confronting his father's ghost? Or Lady Macbeth plotting murder? Or Juliet or Romeo?" But Duncanson persisted with the trial of Shakespeare.

At the 1843 Art Union exhibit this painting soon attracted a crowd. Many people did not know the legend that one of the world's greatest poets and playwrights had once been arrested as a thief. The painting was immediately bought. It is now owned by the Frederick Douglass Community Association of Toledo, Ohio.

Showing a painting is not, however, the same as selling one. Duncanson often had difficulty making ends meet. Occasionally he was given a commission for a portrait by abolitionists such as Freeman Cary or Richard S. Rust, who headed Wilberforce University at that time.

To try to increase his sales, Duncanson went to Detroit, at that time a small city with few artists. There he painted six members of the Berthelet family, one of the city's oldest and wealthiest families. These portraits helped him to obtain other commissions.

Yet he was often without funds. One day he looked so depressed that Henry N. Walker, a prominent merchant who knew his talent, asked what was wrong. "I have been walking the streets not knowing what to do," Duncanson said. "I haven't a penny and I've been turned out of my rooms because I couldn't pay the rent."

"That certainly is too bad," said Mr. Walker.

"If I could get home I'd get some commissions."

"Here, take this," said Mr. Walker, handing him $50. "Get something to eat and go to Cincinnati. Don't worry about paying me back."

Gratefully thanking him, Duncanson hurried to the train. Years later, returning from a successful trip abroad, Duncanson insisted on giving Mr. Walker a fine still life of fruit on a table. It is now in the Detroit Institute of Arts, a gift of Mr. Walker's daughter.

One of the Cincinnatians who became interested in Duncanson's talent—and his difficulties—was Nicholas Longworth, the city's wealthiest man. He invited Duncanson to visit his mansion freely to study his large collection of paintings, engravings, and sculptures. He also commissioned a full-length portrait, one of the best Duncanson ever painted, and stimulated other commissions.

Because he had sponsored the now famous sculptor Hiram Powers, his support of Duncanson impressed many who would otherwise have ignored a Black artist.

In 1851 he sprang a surprise: "Mr. Duncanson, I have a commission to propose. Would you undertake to paint a series of landscapes directly on the plaster of my center hall here at Belmont?"

Duncanson could hardly believe his ears. No artist he knew had ever had such a commission. Together with Mr.

Nicholas Longworth, Cincinnati's best known and wealthiest citizen, aided Duncanson by having him paint landscapes on his mansion's walls and helped him to visit Europe.

Ohio College of Applied Sciences, Cincinnati Art Museum

and Mrs. Longworth he circled the spacious hall. At last he spoke: "I would be delighted to do it!"

Duncanson was months making his sketches and plans. During the actual painting he presumably lived at Belmont. Today these paintings are considered among the finest wall paintings in America and a main feature of Belmont, now the Taft Museum.

Longworth's help did much for Duncanson. The year after he completed his murals, the Art Union showed eight of his paintings. But his family still could not get in to see them. This contradiction, of being accepted in the white world while his family was not, put a great emotional strain on Duncanson. It created a conflict within him that often exhausted him in silent rage or deep depression.

Meanwhile something had happened that hurt all portrait painters: the daguerreotype camera had been developed. By the 1840s it had reached Cincinnati. It produced cheap, accurate "likenesses"—exactly what most people wanted in a portrait. "The daguerreotypes will put us out of portrait painting," said most artists.

Taft Museum, Cincinnati

Duncanson's landscape murals in Longworth's mansion, Belmont, now the Taft Museum, are among the most important examples of this type of work in America.

Interestingly, the most fashionable daguerreotype studio in Cincinnati was that of a lively, quick-witted Black man, J. P. Ball. Originally a waiter, Ball had learned photography from another Black man in Boston and then had come to Cincinnati.

Ball and Duncanson immediately became friends and soon were working together. Ball taught Duncanson how to make daguerreotypes and they joined forces. Six of Duncanson's best landscapes were hung in the main reception room of Ball's studio to create an atmosphere of artistic elegance that other studios could not match.

Ball one day told Duncanson of his plan to create a great historical panorama of Afro-American life.

Panoramas were the newsreels and educational movies of that day. They consisted of strips of canvas, ceiling high, on which dramatic scenes were painted. In the Midwest these strips were sewn together and rolled onto an upright spool. When presented, the room—a hall or theater— was darkened. The scenes on the canvas were illuminated by lamps as the great canvas strip was drawn across a frame onto another spool, creating a "moving picture." A lecturer explained each scene as the canvas unwound. Typical panoramas presented Biblical scenes, views of famous waterfalls, the pyramids of Egypt, or great moments in history.

Duncanson liked Ball's idea and agreed such a panorama would be a success. He pointed out that white people had no idea of the facts about Black people. "That's just it," said Ball. "Here we are—two Black men. We could create something special. No one else will have anything like it. We could put in things that happened right here in Cincinnati, that everybody knows about, like slaves coming across the river. That way we can talk directly to the white people who come to see it."

Thus Ball's famous panorama—nearly a half-mile long—

was created. Although there is no direct proof because
the panorama itself has been lost, it appears logical
that Duncanson, as Ball's close collaborator and an expert
landscapist, directed the scene painters in their work.

Ball's own notes say that the panorama opened with
a sunrise view of an African village, its people going off
on a lion hunt. Later it showed Africans being captured
and carried to America in slave ships. Other scenes showed
slave auctions, plantation work, abuse, and escapes. Some
of the Cincinnati scenes depicted the tragic events of 1829,
1836, and 1841—the mob attacks on Black people, the
wrecking of the abolitionist press, the breaking up of
schools for Black children, the famous trials of fugitive
slaves. The description of the panorama closed with Ball
reciting Longfellow's poem in which the Black people
were compared with "a poor blind Samson" who might
someday "raise his hand and shake the pillars of our com-
monweal, till the vast temple of our liberties, a shapeless
mass of wreck—and rubbish, lies."

Unfortunately this visual history of slavery and Cincinnati as seen by Black men before the Civil War has
been lost. Except for Ball's commentary, its existence
would not ever have been known. One can only guess as to
its artistic merit and its impact.

Duncanson's association with Ball provided a steady in-
come. Shortly after he had come to Mount Pleasant in
1841 he married a young woman who, according to some
sources, had escaped from slavery. She bore him a son,
Reuben. Unfortunately she soon became ill and died.
Reuben was raised by Duncanson's mother. Later, when
Reuben was old enough, Duncanson found him a job in
the city as a clerk.

Gradually Duncanson resumed painting, for he found
daguerreotyping limited. In 1853 he went to Europe with

his good friend William L. Sonntag, a Pennsylvania landscape artist who had come to Cincinnati about the same
time as Duncanson. Sonntag greatly influenced Duncanson's development as a landscape painter.

Duncanson sailed to Europe with a letter from Nicholas
Longworth to Hiram Powers, then considered America's
greatest sculptor, who was living in Italy: "This letter will
be handed to you by Mr. Duncanson, a self-taught artist
of our city. He is a man of integrity and gentlemanly de-
portment, and when you shall see the first landscape he
shall paint in Italy, advise me the name of the artist in
Italy that, with the same experience, can paint so fine a
picture."

Seeing the work of great European masters helped Duncanson gain a new perspective on himself as an artist. He
decided that what he did best was landscape painting.
Thereafter he devoted himself to it, making few portraits.
On his return, he renewed his sketching trips to the West
and visited Niagara Falls and New England.

While visiting Rome, he met the greatest American
actress of the day, Charlotte Saunders Cushman. She was
the friend and confidante of many eminent people. Famous for her Shakespearean roles, in real life she played
an important part in the fight against slavery. She used
her contacts with powerful social and political figures to
aid and draw attention to talented Black artists to demon-
strate how gifted Black people were. Edmonia Lewis, then
an unknown young Black woman from Oberlin College
who had shown talent as a sculptor, was aided in selling her
work in Rome by the actress. Eventually, after studying
the work of Hiram Powers and others, Edmonia Lewis developed into a distinguished neoclassical sculptor whose
work was widely shown in America.

When Miss Cushman saw Duncanson's work, she commissioned him to portray her as Lady Macbeth. Later, in England, she helped to bring him to public attention.

Duncanson's paintings now sold regularly. People as far away as Boston would commission him to paint western landscapes such as the Falls of Minnehaha in Minnesota.

About 1858 Duncanson, who had moved into Cincinnati once Reuben had a job, married again. Before long he and his young wife Phoebe had a son. They named him Milton, after John Milton, one of the English writers Duncanson loved. Later they had a daughter, Bertha. By 1860 Duncanson was fairly well-established; he owned a house worth $3,000 and his personal effects were valued at $800. This indicated a high degree of success in those days.

Well liked by his fellow artists, he enjoyed making the rounds of their studios to see work in progress. He liked to joke that Godfrey and John Frankenstein put so much grass into their landscapes that their paintings had to be hidden lest the cows eat them.

One day in April 1861 Duncanson was at work at his easel when a neighboring artist burst in crying, "The South Carolinians have fired on Fort Sumter! Civil war has begun! My God, Duncanson, you had better flee to Canada. They'll be trying to take Cincinnati!"

"Well, if it's started, I don't think we'll be fleeing to Canada," said Duncanson. "Remember, I came to Cincinnati from Canada. The Black people here will fight, even if no one else does."

With that Duncanson rushed out. He found Peter H. Clark, and other Black leaders working to prepare a defense organization. But what were the white people in Cincinnati going to do? They had often attacked Black homes and their Mayor George Hatch was openly pro-slavery. Would such people simply surrender the city to the Confederate forces when they approached?

Duncanson tried to continue his work on a painting he felt would be his best. Suddenly, an escaping slave brought word that Confederate General Edmund Kirby-Smith had routed the Union forces in Kentucky and was marching toward the Ohio River. He thought Cincinnati was defenseless, a ripe plum that would fall into his lap with a little help from the proslavery forces in the city.

In their churches near the river Black people gathered grimly. They had been collecting arms for weeks. "When they try to cross, we'll try to stop them at the river's edge," they said. Only the abolitionists also prepared for battle.

But nobody in the city—or in the Confederacy—knew the character of Union General Lew Wallace. Ordered to defend Cincinnati, he rode into the city on September 1 with a handful of officers and no troops. He astonished his own officers. "There are 200,000 people here and they can defend themselves," he said. "What they need is leadership." With that he proceeded to lead.

He immediately issued a proclamation calling for a citizens' defense of the city. He closed all businesses, offices, saloons, and stores and stopped all ferry boats. He declared the defense must be carried out "equally by all classes." He ordered the citizens to report for duty assignments on this principle: "Citizens for labor, soldiers for battle." He offered all citizens their choice—fight or work. He wired the governors of Ohio and Indiana for volunteers.

Pro-slavery Mayor Hatch tried to sabotage the plan. He denied that Black men could be considered citizens and told his police to arrest them. His police were the same ones who had often led mobs against the Blacks. Now they searched Black homes for men, arrested all they could find and dragged them into a pen on Plum Street. Later they put them in a stockade on the Kentucky side of the river. (Kentucky, though a slave state, remained loyal to the Union.) Many leading Black men—presumably Duncanson too—escaped by hiding. Others fled to nearby villages and abolitionist centers such as the Lane Seminary. The Black people knew that Mayor Hatch and his police were trying to provoke a race riot that would disrupt defense of the city. They refused to be provoked.

Finally word of what was happening reached General Wallace. He relieved Mayor Hatch and his police of control. He made Judge William M. Dickson, a long time friend of Black Cincinnatians, a colonel and put him in charge of all affairs related to Black people. Judge Dickson ordered every Black man freed and asked them to rejoin their families, assuring them of their safety. Then he called for a "Black Brigade to defend the city."

Many of the men who had been in hiding—perhaps including Duncanson, for there are no adequate records—stepped forward. An American flag with the words "The Black Brigade of Cincinnati" inscribed across it was presented to them with a stirring speech: "Men of the Black Brigade, rally around it. Assert your manhood. Be loyal to duty; be obedient, hopeful, patient. Slavery will soon die; the slave-holders' rebellion, accursed of God and man, will shortly and miserably perish. There will then be, through all the coming ages, in very truth, a land of the free—one country, one flag, one destiny."

The Black Brigade then outdid all other groups in digging fortifications on the hills outside Covington, Kentucky. Meanwhile, into the city flocked volunteers from all over Ohio and Indiana—60,000 of them, armed with everything from horse pistols and ancient muskets to pitchforks. General Wallace got rivermen to assemble a pontoon bridge based on coal barges and his "squirrel hunters" poured across it into the trenches prepared by the Black Brigade and other defense workers.

Desperate, Mayor Hatch then attempted to have General Wallace removed from command, but his plot failed.

Meanwhile, Confederate General Henry Heth, sent by General Kirby-Smith to capture Cincinnati, found himself confronted with amazing fortifications and an astonishing volunteer citizens army. He spent a day inspecting the fortifications, looking for a weak spot. The more he heard from his spies in Cincinnati, the more alarmed he became. His army would be massacred if they attacked—and that night he quietly retreated. Cincinnati was saved!

In the jubilant celebration that followed, the Black Brigade was hailed by other work battalions and by the soldiers for its great work. The fact that the Black men had been initially abused by the police and denied the opportunity to fight was described by speakers at the celebration and by the press. Summing up, the Cincinnati *Gazette* said: "While all have done well, the Negroes as a class must bear away the palm . . . Whenever the men of the Black Brigade appear, they are cheered by our troops."

Duncanson and other Black Cincinnatians returned to their homes with great satisfaction. Two days after the Black Brigade was mustered out, President Lincoln announced that the Emancipation Proclamation would be issued on January 1, 1863.

A great victory celebration in Cincinnati honored General Wallace on October 18. Duncanson and others sought to do his portrait. Wallace, however, strongly favored Duncanson's artist friend, Thomas Buchanan Read, who served as his aide in the city's defense. It may have been through Duncanson and Read that General Wallace had learned how the Black people were being abused by Mayor Hatch's police.

As Cincinnati quieted down, Duncanson returned to work on the painting he felt would be his most important work. It was based on Alfred Tennyson's poem *The Lotos-Eaters*. The poem told the story of the weary, homeward-bound Greek warriors of Odysseus reaching a beautiful and magical island. There, after eating the fruit of the lotos tree, they lost interest in going home, working, or doing anything. They saw life as being "from one sorrow to another thrown," and they wanted only to be left alone on this idyllic island.

Duncanson attempted to portray such an island in *The Land of the Lotos Eaters*. He made several versions. His final version greatly impressed his fellow artists. Exhibited, it attracted large crowds in Cincinnati. Duncanson took it to Canada, then to Glasgow, Edinburgh, and London. Everywhere it met with success. His old acquaintance actress Charlotte Cushman brought many important people to see it. British art journals praised it.

Miss Cushman introduced Duncanson to the Duchess of Sutherland, a member of the nobility and a leading abolitionist in Britain. She arranged for the sale of some paintings and for Tennyson to see *The Land of the Lotos Eaters*. Impressed, Tennyson wrote Duncanson, inviting him to visit his home on the Isle of Wight. Duncanson, in Scotland at the time, was unable to accept.

But he carried the letter with him. In a London museum one day he met an old Cincinnati acquaintance, the Reverend Moncure D. Conway, a Presbyterian abolitionist. "I'm told you have been a great success here," said Rev. Conway.

"Far better than I expected," said Duncanson. "Read this letter." He handed him Tennyson's note.

"You are to be congratulated! This is marvelous. I understand Tennyson has turned down a title from the Queen and won't see the Prime Minister. Yet he invites you to dinner. People in Cincinnati should know Alfred Tennyson wants you to come to supper at his house! It is a shame that you have had to leave your native land to find major recognition," said Conway.

Soon in a letter to the Cincinnati *Gazette*, Rev. Conway told of meeting Duncanson in London, reminded the readers of the artist's struggles in Cincinnati, and described his invitation from Tennyson. To confront Cincinnatians with their prejudice, he wrote: "Think of a Negro sitting at a table with Mr. and Mrs. Alfred Tennyson, Lord and Lady of the Manor, and Mirror of Aristocracy."

Duncanson rejected all chances to sell *The Land of the Lotos Eaters* in England. He visited the Duchess of Sutherland's estate in Scotland, sketching nearby Loch Katrine and its Ellen's Isle many times.

An 1870 version of *Ellen's Isle, Lake Katrine* was promptly purchased by Senator Charles Sumner, the great abolitionist. In 1856 he had been nearly killed on the Senate floor by a Southern congressman, Preston S. Brooks. In trying to regain his health, Sumner had visited the Duchess of Sutherland and seen Loch Katrine. A major art collector, owning great works by Italian masters and many others, he was enchanted by Duncanson's painting. He hung *Ellen's Isle* in his bedroom.

Duncanson, on learning Senator Sumner liked his work, decided to give him his most famous work, *The Land of the Lotos Eaters*. He wanted the gift to be an expression of the gratitude of all Black people for Sumner's courageous fight on their behalf. He went to Boston to make the presentation personally. Perhaps at that time Duncanson may have met Edward M. Bannister, another Black artist. Later, Bannister's landscape *Under the Oaks* won the gold medal first prize at the Philadelphia Centennial Exposition of 1876.

Senator Sumner, while acknowledging the spirit of the

gift, had made it a principle not to accept gifts for what he did as a legislator. He also felt the painting was far more important to Duncanson than it could be to him. Therefore, he reluctantly declined the gift. Duncanson was quite hurt. He renewed his offer in a letter and left the painting with a Boston framer for Sumner. Senator Sumner then said that he would only hold the painting in trust for him.

In 1870–71 Duncanson returned to Scotland on another painting trip. His earlier paintings rendered specific hills, trees and foliage. His new paintings reflected his inner feelings and were more moody, spiritual, and romantic.

When Duncanson returned to the United States he went to Detroit in the fall of 1872. There he suffered a complete physical and nervous breakdown and was hospitalized in a sanitorium. Senator Sumner, learning of his illness, had *The Land of the Lotos Eaters* appraised, added $100 to that sum, and sent the money to Mrs. Duncanson. He also arranged for *Ellen's Isle* ultimately to revert to the Duncanson family.

Duncanson's health continued to fail, and on December 21, 1872, he died. The Detroit *Tribune*, praising his great achievements but not mentioning that he was Black, called him "a man of rare accomplishments" whose death would be regretted by all art lovers. In Cincinnati his old artist friends published a memorial praising him and his work. They understood what he had accomplished as an artist— and had glimpsed the great effort this required for a Black man in the time of slavery.

Today Duncanson's work should establish him as one of the foremost American landscape painters, a Black man who helped to create the first and most distinctly American school of painting—the Hudson River School. Yet his achievement has not yet been fully recognized.

HENRY OSSAWA TANNER
(1859–1937)

Tanner's first religious paintings were skillful but literal illustrations of biblical stories like this one, *Return from the Cross*.

One sunny day in 1873, nearly a hundred years ago, an
adolescent boy and his father, walking in the woods of
Fairmount Park in Philadelphia, unexpectedly came upon
an artist at work. He was painting the scene directly
ahead—a grassy hill with a magnificent towering elm.

The boy and his father moved forward silently. At last
they could see how the artist was applying his colors to
create the distant woods and great elm. The boy whis-
pered, "Can I try to do that?" His father nodded, "Of
course, Henry. Try it and see what happens!"

Next day the boy tacked a piece of old awning to a
board to make a canvas. He found the broken-off back of
an old geography book, punched a hole in it so that he

could wiggle his thumb through it, and thus created a palette for his colors. Then, with a few cheap brushes and tubes of color like those he had seen the artist use—blue, yellow, white, dark brown—he headed for the exact spot where he had seen the artist painting. He worked hard to create the scene on his awning canvas. At last, he managed to capture something of its essence—crudely but enough to show that the hill was a hill, the tree was a tree, the bushes were foliage, the sky was blue. He could do it. He could be a painter, he felt with enormous happiness. He raced home.

Putting his painting down before his mother, he cried, "Look what I've painted. Can you see it?" His mother looked earnestly at his work. At last she said, "Yes, I can see the trees, the grass and the hill."

"I'm an artist! That's what I am now," cried the boy. His brother and sisters gathered around to see his painting. His mother smiled. "I guess you *are* an artist, Henry," she said. She had never seen him so happy. Thus began the career of one of our most outstanding Black artists.

Henry Ossawa Tanner had been born in Pittsburgh on June 21, 1859. In honor of abolitionist John Brown, Henry's father gave Henry the middle name of Ossawa—which was derived from Osawatomie, Kansas, where in 1856 John Brown had first fought proslavery men. A few months after Henry was born, John Brown raided Harpers Ferry in an effort to start an uprising of slaves, for which action, considered treasonable, he was hanged.

Henry Ossawa Tanner's father was an unusual man. Born of free Black parents in Pittsburgh in 1835, he had made himself a college-educated man before the Civil War, by earning his way through Avery College working as a barber. Actively religious, he studied at Western Theological Seminary for three years and was licensed as a minister by the African Methodist Episcopal Church. He saw the Civil War was coming and he wanted to be ready to help Black people find freedom and spiritual peace. Eventually, he became a bishop in the A.M.E. Church and its leading writer and editor. The Reverend Mr. Tanner was a minister in Philadelphia when Henry declared he wanted to be an artist. Characteristically, his father encouraged Henry to try painting. He believed that Black people could succeed at anything.

When Henry was born, he was so small and delicate that his parents feared he would not live. His mother provided the loving care that made it possible for him to survive. Yet he remained a thin, physically frail boy whose poor health tended to make him rather timid and shy. He could not do heavy work or compete in very rough games. This often made him sad.

But painting gave him some confidence in himself. After all he was—an artist. At school, throughout the neighborhood, he told everyone, "I'm an artist. I'm going to paint pictures."

Seeking training, he earnestly knocked at artists' doors. Invariably they turned him down, apparently because of his color. At last, a Mr. Williams accepted him at $2 a lesson, a huge sum to a young minister's son—and the first lesson was simply drawing straight lines. Henry promptly quit. "You'd have to be rich to learn at these prices," he said.

He determined to struggle on alone. He went to the zoo to draw animals. He drew and painted his friends and family. He modeled animals and figures.

Three years after he had first seen the artist in Fairmount Park, the Centennial Exposition was set up there to celebrate the nation's first hundred years, Philadelphia being the birthplace of the nation. A major attraction was an exhibition of the work of artists from all over the world. In the American section Tanner saw a remarkable statue of Cleopatra by Edmonia Lewis, a young Afro-American woman who had become a sculptor in Rome. Young Henry immediately felt attracted to Rome.

Even more impressive to him was the painting *Under the Oaks*, which won a medal for landscape painting. It was the work of a Black artist named Edward M. Bannister who had been a founder of the Providence Art Club in Rhode Island. Bishop Tanner made sure his children saw the work of these Black artists. He considered their work as confirming his firm belief that no accomplishment was beyond his people.

Yet Henry's parents worried about him. He was not interested in anything but painting. How was he ever going to make a living? Finally his father got Henry, then in his late teens, a job as a salesman in a flour mill. The labor was hard and dusty, the working day twelve hours long. In order to paint, Henry got up extra early to paint in a few minutes of daylight before going to the mill. Under the strain of such long, hard hours Henry became very ill with a serious lung condition. He had to rest in the mountains of upper New York State for months. His parents, recognizing that their son was not going to stop trying to be an artist, found a way to support him on his return home.

Now Henry applied for admission to the Pennsylvania Academy of Fine Arts in 1880. One of his teachers was Thomas Eakins, who later would be recognized as one of America's leading painters. However, at this time, Eakins was considered one of the finest teachers in the nation. He accepted Henry in his studio class. Eakins believed you should paint what you saw around you in America: baseball players, surgeons, oarsmen, hunters—not ancient historical scenes or romanticized symbolic figures.

Under Eakins' guidance, Henry's talent thrived. One day, after he had made a start that was better than anything he had done before, Eakins praised the work and urged him to go on with it. But Henry, afraid he would ruin his painting by trying to improve it, wasted several days doing nothing.

Seeing no progress, Eakins was disgusted. "What have you been doing?" he demanded. "Get it—get it better or get it worse! No middle ground or compromise!"

This demand that he risk failure to achieve a goal was an important lesson to Henry. He remembered it all his life and it became a guide for him in many situations.

Yet Henry was often deeply hurt by abuse and humiliation from students who did not accept him.

After two years, he gave up the Eakins class, feeling he had learned the essentials of painting. He made trips to the Jersey shore to paint the dunes. He did landscapes and portraits of his father and mother. The famous Bishop Daniel A. Payne, who developed Wilberforce University,

Harmon Foundation, New York City

Henry Ossawa Tanner's mother and father supported him during his long, difficult struggle. His father, a bishop of the A.M.E. Church during the period after the Civil War, deeply influenced Tanner's thinking and art.

bought three of his paintings. He constantly sent drawings to New York publishers and sometimes sold one.

His work was exhibited at the Pennsylvania Academy of Fine Arts annual shows, and once he won a prize for a study of a lion. However, his work was seldom bought.

Several discouraging years passed. He was depressed that he was unable to support himself.

One day Henry got a "bright idea," as he called it, for making a living. Eakins had stimulated his interest in photography. Why not open a portrait photo studio in Atlanta, Georgia? He knew that city had a large, relatively prosperous Black population, that it was a major center of Black colleges and businesses. He already knew faculty members at Clark College in Atlanta. With a photo studio there, he confidently expected to make enough money to have considerable time to paint. Therefore, in the summer of 1888, he moved to Atlanta. But the studio was a dismal failure. After a year he was in even worse financial trouble.

Fortunately, a friend introduced him to Bishop and Mrs. Joseph L. Hartzell of Cincinnati. The Hartzells were white. They had spent years in Africa as missionaries and had a deep appreciation of African art and culture.

On seeing Tanner's paintings, they rescued him from his photo studio by having him appointed art instructor at Clark College in Atlanta. Before the college opened that fall Tanner made a camera tour of the North Carolina highlands. He photographed cottages for their owners and made picture postcards. Both sold well. In the highlands, he also made many sketches of its people. At the college he soon had commissions for portraits and gave lessons in drawing to faculty members.

When Bishop and Mrs. Hartzell learned that he hoped to study art in Rome, where Edmonia Lewis had succeeded,

Mrs. Hartzell decided to help him by arranging a show of his paintings in Cincinnati. Had not Duncanson been successful there?

The show lasted three weeks—but not a single painting was sold. To prevent Tanner from being utterly discouraged the Hartzells bought the entire collection for $300. This enabled him to sail to Europe in early 1891.

En route to Rome, Henry decided to stop in Paris to see its museums and art schools. That decision was to change his life. At the Académie Julien, one of its best schools, Henry was caught up in the enthusiasm of its students. He was impressed that one of the leading painters of France, Benjamin Constant, was teaching there—and that he himself could enroll without any difficulty about his being Black. The students were warm and friendly toward him. How unlike the United States! In this stimulating atmosphere, Tanner felt himself grow. He worked hard and he was popular. He won a student drawing competition. He soon won the considered attention of Constant who presently gave Tanner his photograph, writing on it: "To my pupil and friend Tanner, always confident of his ultimate success." Young Henry felt he had at last found an artistic home.

Henry hoped eventually to enter his work in the great exhibit of École des Beaux-Artes, commonly called the Paris Salon. As many as 10,000 persons a day paid to see the Salon. This enormous competitive exhibit was a main avenue to success for many an artist. Merely to be accepted by the Salon jury was important to a young artist. But Henry's paintings were not accepted.

Trying to stretch his dollars by eating very little over a period of several years, he had weakened his body's defenses. He became desperately ill with typhoid fever. In the hospital he gradually recovered, but he was too weak to take care of himself. One thing was clear: to survive, he had to go home. Friends shipped his canvases.

Back home in America in the fall of 1892, ill and weak, his goals still to be achieved, Tanner felt depressed. His family and friends welcomed him. Under his mother's care, eating her good food regularly, he began to feel better. "If worse comes to worse, always remember you have a home," she had often told him.

He enjoyed, during his slow recovery, renewing his closeness to his family. His oldest sister had become a physician. His young brother was becoming a minister. Two other sisters had married ministers and were raising families.

But he also had many things to reflect on. His life abroad had given him a new perspective on America, on prejudice, on the way his father's profound and assertive faith had sustained the family and the members of his church in the midst of turmoil and cruel racial discrimination. Indeed, despite severe difficulties, the A.M.E. church had grown and his father had become a bishop.

Having encountered many religious faiths and even more nationalities in Paris, Henry Tanner had learned that prejudice even distorts white people's views of one another. Why couldn't there be an end to all prejudice? Why couldn't there be a Christian brotherhood of man? Why couldn't there be an end to hate and violence? Such thoughts were stimulated by his renewed contact with racial prejudice in Philadelphia where most restaurants refused to serve a Black person. He was surprised to find himself thinking of Paris as his "home," a place where one did not encounter such virulent racism.

But his thoughts about religion and prejudice drifted off as his strength returned and he began to paint again, touching up the canvases sent from France. Working once

more from his old sketches from the North Carolina
highlands, he completed *The Banjo Lesson* in the style
that Eakins taught. It shows a human, dignified, aspect of
life among Black people—an old man patiently teaching
a young boy how to play the banjo. It refuted the caricatures
of Black people in wide circulation at that time and impressed those who saw it. Tanner was urged to stay in
America and continue such work. But the art center of
the world was Paris and he felt that he had to prove
himself there.

Henry grew almost desperate to return to France,
which he felt was his artistic home. To raise funds quickly,
he auctioned off his paintings and drawings—literally everything he could lay his hands on. One of the paintings sold
was *The Banjo Lesson*, which eventually found its way
to the Hampton Institute in Virginia.

With the money from the sale, he quickly returned
to Paris. What he had just seen in the United States—
what he remembered of racial prejudice in Atlanta, in
Philadelphia, in New Jersey—made him determined to
renew his efforts to prove he could reach the highest levels
of the art world. He was therefore delighted to find that
his new paintings were accepted by the Salon jury.

Yet Tanner recognized that as a painter he now faced
a crisis; his long apprenticeship was over. He saw that
his work lacked a completely personal style and viewpoint,
something that would make it both recognizable and distinguished. Like many artists, he had simply been painting
picturesque landscapes, seascapes, fishermen and their
boats, apple orchards in blossom, shoemakers, all in a
rather photographic way.

Nothing he had painted so far, Tanner also realized,
expressed his innermost feelings or the vision of the world
that was taking shape within him, a vision inseparable

from his spiritual and religious background. Could he not express in some symbolic yet artistic manner, his hopes, his dreams of salvation, of freedom, of peace?

He turned to religious painting. He had often discussed such art with his father, who always observed that religious themes had provided great artists like Rembrandt and Michelangelo with enduring subjects through the centuries. It was not hard for Tanner to recognize that the persecution of the early Christians was very much like the oppression and persecution of his own people.

Out of the many subjects crowding his mind, he decided to start with a biblical story—Daniel in the lions' den. He went to the Paris zoo and drew lions by the hour, until he knew exactly how they stalked forward, lay down, waited with switching tails, held their heads, crouched, and pounced on their meals. He even went to Emmanuel Frémiet, the leading French animal sculptor, and studied under him, modeling lions in clay.

At last he felt ready for the painting he had in mind. He painted a deep, dark dungeon with lions restlessly stalking in the shadows. Quietly, at peace with himself, without fear, Daniel leans back against a masonry projection in their midst. Only moonlight, coming through a hole in the dungeon ceiling, lights the scene, hitting Daniel's hands and robe and a waiting lion's paw. But the upper part of his body and head are in shadow. This dramatic use of light, similar to Rembrandt's, was to become characteristic of Tanner's work. It has a symbolic meaning. One might say that in Tanner's paintings light stands for man's hope and salvation. Just such hope carried this frail, shy Black young man through enormous struggles and against all odds—and would carry him still further.

Entered in the great Paris Salon of 1895. *Daniel in the Lions' Den* was awarded an honorable mention. Visitors took note of it. The art critics mentioned it. Tanner at last felt he had found a way in which he could excel and develop a unified style and viewpoint.

The recognition this painting won, he later wrote, gave him "a courage and a power for work, and also a hope that I had never before possessed."

Yet recognition again brought pressure on Tanner to come home and paint American subjects—not Daniel in the lions' den.

Some Black leaders, including Booker T. Washington, who had seen *The Banjo Lesson,* came to Paris. They sought to get Tanner to devote himself to more such portraits. But Tanner, who had been stifled in America, was firm about his need to remain in Europe. Although disappointed, Washington accepted Tanner's view. He recognized that Tanner must do what was best for himself as an artist.

Tanner promptly began preparing for the next Salon, making studies for another biblical painting, *The Raising of Lazarus.* This time he sought as models, men and women whose faces seemed to match the characters in the biblical story. It was a small painting. But it immediately excited Benjamin Constant and other friends. Rodman Wanamaker, of the wealthy Philadelphia department store family, heard of it and asked to see it. Impressed, he immediately offered to pay Tanner's expenses for a six-week tour of the Holy Land, something Tanner had dreamed of for many years.

Before leaving, Tanner made sure his picture was delivered to the Salon. In the Holy Land, he found great new stimulation. He was much impressed by the barren landscape. It seemed to him to be the natural setting of a great tragedy. He sketched the wilderness, the market places, and found as models persons with old Hebraic faces. He sketched shepherds, carpenters, fishermen, and other types mentioned in the Bible—young women, mothers, children, old women. He sketched old costumes, architecture, landscapes as authentic guides for later work.

While traveling, Tanner received an official letter from the French government. It offered to buy *The Raising of Lazarus* for the Luxembourg Museum in Paris. Such an offer was one of the prizes of the Salon, accompanied by a medal. Tanner could scarcely believe his eyes. Because the letter had been mailed three weeks earlier, he feared the offer was by now void. He ran to the telegraph office and sent a wire of acceptance so long that it "almost broke the bank," he said later.

Next day he received letters from artist friends congratulating him. One letter said only: "Come home, Tanner, to see the crowds before your picture."

Tanner left promptly for Paris. Just as his friend had written, crowds of people were standing before his painting. He was besieged for interviews. The *Ladies Home Journal* commissioned him to portray famous women in the Bible. Newspapers all over the world reproduced *The Raising of Lazarus* and told their readers how—less than forty years after slavery—a Black American had won one of the world's great art prizes. Only a few Americans had won such attention, one being James McNeill Whistler, for his famous portrait of his mother. Yet none of these artists had to overcome the racial prejudice that frail Henry Ossawa Tanner had conquered.

After that, Tanner was accorded many great honors. Once again, in 1906, the French government purchased a work of his, *Disciples at Emmaus* at four times the price paid for *The Raising of Lazarus*. In the Salon, Tanner's painting competed with those of the best-known artists of that day.

Collection of Mr. & Mrs. Erwin S. Barrie

Tanner made this etching from one of his studies for *The Raising of Lazarus*, his first painting to win a major prize in the famous Paris Salon.

Many museums and collectors in the United States bought Tanner's paintings, and he won notable prizes in this country, including the Walter Lippincott prize at Pennsylvania Academy of Fine Arts where he had once been miserable as a student. The Chicago Art Institute and Pittsburgh's Carnegie Institute Museum of Arts were among those purchasing his work. One of the collectors who bought his work was Atherton Curtis, American heir to a patent medicine fortune. He became one of Tanner's closest friends.

Each time Tanner exhibited or won a new prize, the press carried the story of this Black artist's triumphant struggle.

Meanwhile Tanner had married Jessie Olsen of San Francisco whom he met while she was studying operatic singing in Europe. She posed for one of his most famous paintings, *The Annunciation,* now in the Philadelphia Museum of Art. Their only child, Jesse Ossawa Tanner, was born in New York during the couple's short, unsuccessful attempt to live there. After that Tanner and his family stayed abroad except for short visits here. He had a studio in Paris and another at Trepied, an art colony on the Brittany coast. There he headed the society of artists and he and his wife enjoyed the company of many friends.

Tanner's art was based on his idealized, mystical concept of the brotherhood of man under Christ. Suddenly these ideals were shattered by the ugly realities of World War I with both sides proclaiming God was on their side. Refugees and Allied soldiers poured into Trepied as the German armies advanced.

The Tanners had to flee from Trepied. But it was the spiritual, rather than the physical, hardship of the war that devastated Tanner. A sensitive, gentle man, opposed

to violence all his life, he was unable to work. War was
the opposite of what he sought in portraying the Prince
of Peace as a radiant light. He drafted a despondent
note to his friend Atherton Curtis: "Only once in a
while, thank God, does one realize the suffering and despair that is contained in a sentence like 40 killed, 400
killed, 4000 missing, 40,000 losses. How many loving,
carefully raised sons in that number, how many fathers,
how many lonely wives, mothers, children, sweethearts,
waiting for the return that never comes. This waiting—
how hard it is—how much harder than action, waiting,
waiting, with less light each day until despair puts out
all light of life—and this is why I cannot work . . ."

As the war dragged on, Tanner's despondency deepened.
After the United States entered the war in April 1917,
Tanner sought to overcome his despair by becoming
actively involved—not in fighting, for he was fifty-seven
years old, but by helping the wounded. Having often been
sick himself, he knew that planting seeds, watching tiny
shoots develop into plants with cultivation helped pass
time and raised one's spirits. He conceived the idea of
using vacant fields around base hospitals to make vegetable
gardens that could be tended by convalescing soldiers.
Convincing American Red Cross officials of its soundness,
Tanner was commissioned to establish the project. This
he did brilliantly—even raising livestock as well as supply-
ing hospitals with fresh vegetables. More important, the
activity relieved the tension, anxiety, and frustration of
hundreds of recovering soldiers, many of them shell-
shocked. It also lifted some of the despondency Tanner felt
by making him feel useful. He decided to do some sketching in the Red Cross canteens at the front.

But Tanner was not able to idealize the war or its
soldiers. The figures in these paintings are stiff, without

color or warmth. There is no hope in them or their setting. In a certain deep sense he could not respond to this situation. For while thousands of Black American soldiers were fighting in United States uniforms in this war to "make the world safe for democracy" to guarantee their democratic right, he knew that other Americans were determined not to give them their rights. Among his "jottings," as he called his notes, he recorded how an American captain told of the heroic exploits of a Black regiment in fighting but then concluded, "but we will have to kill several of those niggers down home before we will be able to get them back in their place."

When peace at last came, Tanner was slow in starting to paint again. The war had profoundly altered the values by which men guided themselves. It had not made the world safe for democracy. Secret treaties had emerged at the peace table and it was now clear that profiteering had often been disguised as patriotism. Disillusion set in everywhere. People found it hard to have faith in anything.

Tanner himself, as a religious painter, had felt this shift in values before the outbreak of the war. But he had not expected the painters of the Salon to be swept away—and the art world to be dominated by—the prewar rebels, Picasso, Braque, Matisse. And everywhere new ideas in art such as Cubism were increasingly in vogue. All the aesthetic values of the Salon painters—correct perspective, anatomy, light and shade, figurative painting, and likeness in portraiture—were cast aside. Instead the moderns valued color harmonies and rhythms, a search for mood and intense inner emotion of the subject, and in the case of the Cubists, analysis of the subject in terms of planes. The work of the Cubists especially irritated the older academic painters who felt such work was fragmented and irrational.

Joshua Johnston, America's first significant Black artist, painted this portrait of an unknown cleric about 1810. It may be a portrait of the Reverend Daniel Coker, an outstanding leader of Black people in Baltimore at the time that Johnston worked there.

Bowdoin College Museum of Art, Brunswick, Me.

Henry M. Fuller, New York City

Although considered a painter of the Hudson River School, which concentrated on scenes of America's untamed and unpolluted wilderness, Robert S. Duncanson also painted idyllic scenes, such as the painting above, Romantic Landscape.

Blue Hole, Flood Waters, Little Miami River was painted by Robert S. Duncanson, a Black artist who was prominent in Cincinnati before the Civil War. This swampy locale was a favorite hiding place for fugitive slaves, offering easy concealment.

The Banjo Lesson, *based on Henry O. Tanner's southern sketches, portrays the transmission of Black America's musical heritage from one generation to another with dignity.*

Tanner's On the Road to Bethany *has never been shown in this country. It displays his skillful use of light to express his mystic hope for mankind.*

John Brown Going to His Hanging *is based on Pippin's grand-mother's account of that incident. She was present, so Pippin painted her sad face from memory on the right, looking directly at the viewer. Some commentators say she represents· Black people turning away from this tragedy.*

Cabin Interior, which Horace Pippin created from his own memory and the stories of his grandmother, portrays the life of Black people with warmth and dignity.

When young, Jacob Lawrence painted grim, unhappy, often violent scenes. When older, he painted joyous scenes, such as Parade, based on a Harlem event. With bright colors and rhythmic patterns, he maintains his identification with Black people.

Slowly, laboriously, preparing many studies, Tanner returned to painting. The war showed its impact in his work. His painting was even more mystical, less defined, more like the work of another great mystic—the American painter Albert Pinkham Ryder.

Further honors and recognition came to him. In 1923 the French government made him a Chevalier of the Legion of Honor. His work was exhibited in New York, Boston, Chicago, and Des Moines. When the Metropolitan Museum of Art in New York indicated that it would like to have a Tanner, his old friend Atherton Curtis presented the museum with a major work, *Sodom and Gomorrah*. Its presence in the Metropolitan inspired many younger Black artists. Tanner came to New York to attend to his exhibits. He also visited his family and his old friend, W. E. B. Du Bois, who was constantly trying to stimulate the development of Black artists through *Crisis*, the National Association for the Advancement of Colored People magazine which he edited.

On returning to France, Tanner found that his wife had developed a fatal lung disease. She died within a few months, on September 8, 1925. Her death left Tanner so depressed that he was unable to work for two years.

Then a new blow fell. In 1929 the stock market in New York collapsed. The economic depression that followed spread to Europe. The unemployed in America numbered more than twelve million. Few people could buy paintings. Tanner found his money was worth half what it had been. He felt lucky to sell a painting once priced at $1,500 for $400. Some patrons no longer had the money to pay for paintings they had ordered.

By 1933 he was seventy-four years old and not in good health. To an artist friend he complained of "struggling to make a picture, and struggling to sell it."

With the Depression, Tanner's painting went "out of style." Museums no longer showed his work. The new modern art forms—Cubism and `Surrealism—were now welcomed in America, stimulating creation of the now famous Museum of Modern Art in New York City. In the 1940s the Metropolitan quietly sold *Sodom and Gomorrah*.

Yet Tanner had been, and continued to be, a major influence on young Black artists. Some traveled to France to see him. William Eduardo Scott studied with Tanner in the 1920s. Others who came included William H. Johnson, Palmer Hayden, Elizabeth Prophet, Hale Woodruff, who later painted murals of the *Amistad* mutiny, and James A. Porter, who became head of the art department of Howard University. They sought his personal encouragement, which he gave warmly.

On May 26, 1937, Tanner died quietly in his sleep in Paris. The newspapers, which had seldom mentioned him for ten years, startled their readers with long obituaries of this Black artist who had conquered the art world of Paris forty years before. But after his death he was quietly forgotten, so much so that many young Black artists in the fifties did not know his name.

But in 1967, following the stimulus of a major show of work by Black artists at City University of New York, Erwin S. Barrie, who had been Tanner's dealer, presented a large Tanner show at Grand Central Art Galleries. He obtained from Tanner's son, Jesse, seventy-five unknown paintings, most of which "were small sketches of a free personal direct kind that may represent Henry Tanner at his best," said John Canaday, art critic of the New York *Times*.

In a critical review Canaday called for a new look at the work of this long neglected artist. This review helped

Archives of American Art, Detroit and New York City

Henry Ossawa Tanner, the first Black artist to win coveted prizes at the Paris Salon, made his first palette from the old, worn-out cover of a geography book.

stimulate the formation of a major collection of Tanner's work for exhibition at the National Collection of Fine Arts in the Smithsonian Institution in Washington in 1969. The exhibition was sent on a transcontinental tour, which included some of America's great museums.

Once again, people were standing before Tanner's paintings, seeing them in a new light—as the work of a major American artist.

HORACE PIPPIN
(1888–1946)

Phillips Collection, Washington, D.C.

The Domino Players was one of the pleasant memory paintings that Pippin made of his childhood days in upstate New York and Pennsylvania.

On a spring day in 1937 two old friends were taking a walk in West Chester, a small town near Philadelphia. They were an art critic, Dr. Christian Brinton, and N. C. Wyeth, a famous illustrator. In the window of the shoe repair shop they saw a painting with strong, flat colors. It was painted on a thick board instead of canvas. The shape of various items appeared to be cut deeply into the painting. Its simple, charming quality caused Dr. Brinton and Mr. Wyeth to inquire about its creator.

"Oh, that was painted by Horace Pippin," said the

shoemaker. "A Black man with a bad arm. He paints all the time. He asked if he could put it in my window. He said, 'Maybe someone would like to buy it.' God knows he needs the money."

Dr. Brinton went to Pippin's home. There he met a tall, dignified, sad-faced man whose right arm hung limply at his side. He could not shake hands except by reaching over with his left arm, seizing his right wrist and lifting the right arm. Then his right hand came alive, full of strength. "My arm got hurt in the war," he said simply.

Dr. Brinton saw more of Pippin's paintings. All had the same brilliant color, painted flatly on boards. He also saw some unfinished paintings—boards with the outlines of figures burned into them. Horace Pippin explained that he drew on a board with a red-hot poker. He showed how he had to support his limp right hand with his left when brush painting on canvas. But with a poker, he could let the heavy iron support his hand and could manipulate it with the pressure of his arm.

Dr. Brinton knew that he had found a great artist. Pippin had already shown his work at the local West Chester Community Center's annual show, but Dr. Brinton set out to arouse the art world. He alerted Holger Cahill, then associated with the Museum of Modern Art in New York. In June 1938 Cahill put four Pippin paintings into a museum exhibit entitled "Masters of Popular Painting."

Dr. Brinton then interested a young Philadelphia dealer, Robert Carlen, a former painter. In 1940 Carlen set about presenting Pippin's first one-man show. But before the paintings could be hung, Dr. Albert C. Barnes, one of America's most influential and wealthy collectors, happened accidentally to see them. Enormously impressed and believing Pippin was America's first Black artist, Dr.

Barnes immediately bought some of the paintings on the spot, including one for actor Charles Laughton.

Dr. Barnes insisted on discarding the already printed catalogue for the show so that he could write an introduction that would herald Pippin's work. This immediately attracted critics, art magazines, collectors, magazines, and columnists to the Pippin show. Museums followed.

Thus fame came to Horace Pippin, who made his first painting at the age of forty-three.

But Pippin was not really interested in fame. He was interested in expressing what was in his mind and heart.

Pippin was an artistic genius. Because his work lacked the finishing touches of highly schooled artists, he was "naïve" and "primitive." But his sense of design and color was elegant and modern. Within a few years, leading museums were boasting they owned "a Pippin." And within a few years Pippin was dead. Few artists ever achieved his high standing in so short a time.

Friday magazine, New York City

Drawing on a board with a hot poker by the kitchen stove, Horace Pippin, whose wrist and arm were hurt badly in World War I, became an outstanding artist.

Horace Pippin was born in West Chester, Pennsylvania, on February 22, 1888. When his mother got work in Goshen, New York, they moved there. Horace grew up in this pleasant village, later famous for its trotting races. He went to the Merry Green Hill School, a one-room schoolhouse where a single teacher taught all the children.

Horace discovered very early that he could draw. At school he would print a word—and then draw a picture of the object: a dog, a cat, a dishpan, a cup, and so on. This annoyed the busy teacher. She made him stay after school to do the lesson "the right way." Later Horace said, "This happened frequently and I just couldn't help it. The worst part of it was, I would get a beating when I got home, for coming home late, regardless of what I was kept in for."

One day Horace saw a magazine advertisement with a cartoon of a funny face. "Draw Me—and win a prize!" said the ad. Horace made a drawing and sent it in. A week later he received the prize—a box of six crayons, a box of water colors, and two brushes.

Delighted, Horace drew and colored pictures of what he saw in the village: houses, stores, trees, and animals. He also copied pictures from Sunday School papers.

Each year the Sunday School held a festival and everyone was asked to donate something to be sold. Horace bought a yard of muslin and cut it up into six pieces. Then he fringed the edges of the pieces to make them look like doilies. On each he drew a biblical scene, such as Jesus ascending, Moses and the fiery bush, Elijah ascending in the chariot of fire, Daniel in the lions' den. He colored them brightly and took them to the festival as his donation. They delighted the ladies in charge, who hung them on a wire to be sold.

All the children were called to get refreshments. When Horace came back, his Sunday School teacher said his doilies had been sold. Excited, he raced off to tell his mother, who was pleased. She knew how hard he had worked on them.

A month later, as Horace was going to school, a lady standing in her doorway called to him. "Aren't you Horace Pippin?"

"Yes, ma'am."

"Are you the one who made the doilies?"

"Yes."

"Well, you certainly made some bum things," she said. She pulled out from under her apron some clean pieces of fringed muslin. "I bought this at the festival with a picture on it. Then I washed it and this is all I have— a piece of muslin."

"But you're not supposed to wash it," protested Horace. "It's only a crayon picture and that washes right off." He went on to school, feeling very unhappy. His feelings were hurt because the lady had implied he had cheated her. Even forty years later he recalled the incident.

Mrs. Pippin then began working at hotels in the Catskill Mountains. Horace went to country schools. When he was fourteen years old, he got a job at a farm owned by James Gavin. One night Mr. Gavin fell asleep while reading his paper. Horace sketched him as he slept and put his drawing on the kitchen table. When Mr. Gavin woke up, he saw the drawing. "Who drew this?" he asked.

"I did," said Horace.

"That's a very good drawing," said Mr. Gavin. "You ought to go to school to really learn. You have the talent."

"Yes, sir," said Horace. "But I have no money."

"Well, maybe I could send you," said Mr. Gavin.

But before inquiries could be made Horace was sum-

moned to Goshen. His mother had gone there and become
seriously ill and was without money. Horace saw that he'd
have to go to work. "Don't worry," he told his mother.
"I'll be able to get a regular job. I'm a good worker."

Thus, at fifteen years of age, Horace Pippin went to
work unloading coal. Then he worked at a feed store.
One day when he was eighteen, he heard they needed a
porter at the local hotel. His friends said, "Horace, you
won't last three weeks." But he was there for seven years,
during which time, in 1911, his mother died.

In 1913 Horace went to Paterson, New Jersey. He
packed and loaded furniture on vans for shipment all
over the country. In 1916 he went to work for American
Brake Shoe Company in nearby Mahwah, hoping to become a moulder in its foundry, a highly skilled worker.

But when the United States entered World War I,
Horace quit to join the army.

Enlisting had an extraordinary meaning to Horace
Pippin. So did everything that happened to him as a
soldier. More than twenty years later he could recall in
detail, almost day by day, what happened. He recounted
this in four autobiographical essays.

Horace joined a unit of Black soldiers that reached
France in December 1917. There, his unit was transferred
to the French command as the 369th Regiment. He and
his comrades were given French rifles instead of American
Springfields and sent into action. He worked to become
a good soldier and was promoted to corporal. For three
months this regiment took a terrible pounding from the
German troops. Its exhausted survivors were then rested
for two weeks. Then they again bore the brunt of a savage
German attack. Still Pippin found time now and then
to make sketches of his buddies and of the landscape.

As corporal, Horace Pippin often bravely served at a

lonely listening post far out in "no man's land." Its purpose was to detect enemy movements and protect the main body of troops against surprise attacks. Men assigned to the outpost were often killed.

Pippin's unit was shifted from place to place, but always kept in the front lines. "For months I didn't know what day it was or what month it was and at this present time I couldn't tell, but the weather acted like October."

One night they were moved into a new sector of the front lines. They were told that they were "going over the top at daybreak." Shortly after dawn, following a heavy artillery bombardment, Pippin's company climbed over the top of its trenches and charged. German machine guns cut men down, but by crawling, creeping, and digging in, they advanced. At noon the French artillery moved up and again blasted the German positions. Again Corporal Pippin led his men forward.

At daybreak Pippin's unit started to advance again, but was driven back by heavy machine-gun fire until the German positions were flanked. Everywhere men were falling dead and wounded. "We wished we could help the wounded but we couldn't. We had to leave them there and keep advancing, ducking from shell hole to shell hole all day. That night I counted fourteen machine-gun nests out of order in our path. The next morning came like the rest, but the machine-gun fire wasn't as heavy as it was before. But the snipers were plentiful. I remember spotting a shell hole and made a run for it. Just as I was within three feet and getting ready to dive in I was hit in the shoulder."

Corporal Pippin fell into the shell hole amid three other soldiers. One bound his wound. Then they left him, moving forward. When Pippin tried to crawl out, a sniper's shots drove him back. A French rifleman came by. Pippin gestured to him to get down. But the French soldier moved too slowly. The sniper killed him almost instantly. Then another French soldier came by and saw his friend dead. When Pippin motioned for him to get down, he jumped into the shell hole with Pippin. Another French soldier then shot the German sniper.

Two stretcher bearers eventually found Pippin, carried him out of the hole, and laid him beside a path. "It started to rain that morning about nine and it rained all day and at night it increased. My stretcher was full of water. About 10 o'clock that night reinforcements were coming up. I could hear them splashing in the mud. Some nearly stepped on me." Finally the new troops sent their stretcher-bearers to take Pippin to a first aid station.

"The next morning I woke up and dead men were on both sides of me. They were carrying the wounded out and leaving the dead in the dugout. It was still raining."

Finally he was taken to a base hospital. Not much could now be done for his wounded arm. Eventually Corporal Pippin reached America on a hospital ship in January 1919. He was discharged on May 22. "My right arm was bound to me. I could not use it for anything," he later recalled. Every man in the 369th Regiment was awarded the Croix de Guerre in honor of its heroic service. Its Black soldiers and officers had spent 191 days in the front lines, five days more than any other U.S. troops. This was something Pippin was proud of all his life.

Pippin went back to West Chester, where he still had relatives. He thought that getting used to life with a shattered arm would be easier there. The government provided a small disability pension, for it was clear that there was little work he could do—certainly not furniture packing or foundry moulding.

He met Jennie Ora Featherstone Wade, a widow with

a young son. Tender and motherly, she spontaneously tried to make Horace comfortable. A year later they married. Mrs. Pippin took in washing to help support the family because Horace's pension was so small. Horace got odd jobs from time to time and delivered the washing.

But mostly he sat, holding his wounded arm in his lap and remembering his particular images of war: how the coal tender had struck the ship before they sailed; how he had posted his guards; the sight of a bombed-out town; his Black buddies in their bunks; the quiet soldier who had known he was not coming back before they went "over the top"; the loneliness and fear in a listening-post assignment in no man's land; the bursting shells; the charging Germans; the gas attacks and how grotesque his buddies looked in their masks. He remembered the way he and his whole Black American regiment were put in the French army, then ordered into one battle after another, until they were nearly all dead or wounded like himself. It all seemed such a waste of effort, and lives.

As a strong man, he missed not being able to work at things he knew how to do. Most of all he missed not being able to draw, the way he had expressed himself from boyhood. He recalled the pictures he made in France. He wished he had them. He could show people then what it was like in the war. Sometimes, holding his right arm in his left hand, he could support his right hand so that his fingers could sketch a few lines. But, his hand tended to smudge the drawing—and he remembered the woman who complained that his doily drawings washed out.

Thus nine years passed. Jennie's son grew up in that time.

One day, in the winter of 1929, Horace Pippin saw the poker in the kitchen coal stove grow red hot. It gave him an idea. He took an oakwood leaf from the dining room table and set it up with its rough bottom side facing him.

Then he took the red-hot poker in his right hand. By supporting that hand with his left hand, he slowly drew on the oak board. He burned into the board the outline of a lonely bent man leading a horse which pulled a covered two-wheeled wagon through the snow. He left the oak untouched to represent the snow. He burned in lines indicating the edge of the woods and the darkness of night. In the foreground he added a fallen log with twisted branches. At the bottom he burned in the title in capitals: *LOSING THE WAY*, and added "By Horace Pippin." He had made a picture, in spite of the war and his limp arm and everything that had happened to him. He had freed himself at last.

Use of the poker strengthened his arm muscles. He was proud of "my invention," as he smilingly referred to his drawing with the poker. The burnt wood panel was the basis of one of his most famous paintings. It was something he had thought about for years—the coming of peace on the battlefield. He called it *The End of the War: Starting Home.* He worked on it for three years. He piled one coat of paint on top of another until at last it was thick with paint, so much so that it appears almost carved. And instead of making an ordinary picture frame, Pippin carved grenades, tanks, bombs, rifles, bayonets, and gas masks into a heavy frame.

In the painting, German soldiers are emerging from trenches and dugouts to surrender to Black soldiers, amid a tangle of barbed wire in a great thicket of bare trees before a desolate mountain. In the sky, bombs burst and planes fall in flames. It is a hauntingly grim picture, the faces of all the soldiers without expression. No one looks

The End of the War was what Pippin called this painting. Obsessed with the tragic waste of life and the pain brought by war, Pippin worked on this painting for three years. He carved the frame and made it part of the painting.

triumphant. The earth itself appears destroyed. This picture of utter destruction and desolation, so patiently and intensely worked over by a man wounded and disabled in the war, is a profound antiwar painting. In it everything is destroyed. Even the end of the war is not a triumph for the victors.

In the next few years Pippin created four more war paintings. In each one he showed the life of Black soldiers. The eloquence of these paintings does not lie in horrible scenes of slaughter, but in their direct, grim portrayal of the desolation of the world.

Because of his injured arm Pippin could not paint with spontaneous brush strokes. His work was preconceived and extraordinary in design and color. Once he wrote about it in this way:

How I Paint: The colors are very simple such as brown, amber, yellow, black, white, and green. The pictures which I have already painted come to me in my mind, and if to me it is a worthwhile picture, I paint it. I go over that picture in my mind several times and when I am ready to paint it I have all the details that I need. I take my time and examine every coat of paint very carefully and to be sure that the exact color I have in mind is satisfactory to me. Then I work my foreground from the background. That throws the background away from the foreground. In other words, bringing out my work.

These are not the comments of a naïve, simple, uneducated man. They show a profound understanding of painting—and a determination to carry it out despite his injured arm. What it took was an enormously patient person willing to search endlessly for the right color, for an appropriate design or composition.

Pippin had painted in quiet solitude for nearly nine years before Dr. Brinton saw his work. In those years he eased his mind of his painful memories of the war by painting them. He also recalled, in other paintings, scenes from Goshen and other childhood memories.

When his paintings began to attract attention he was pleased. He was appreciative of the friendship and interest in him which his paintings brought. However fame itself did not interest him. His great integrity kept him at ease and comfortable amid wealthy art collectors and noted art critics. His work continued to get better.

Dr. Brinton, whose portrait he painted, tried to tell him how to paint. Pippin coolly rejected his advice. The only advice he accepted was that of young Robert Carlen who had been an artist before becoming a dealer in Philadelphia. Carlen not only gave Pippin his first one-man show in 1940, but kept him supplied with materials and maintained close contact with him.

Dr. Barnes, who had written an essay on the potential development of the Black artists in America for Dr. Alain Locke's book, *The New Negro*, felt that his prophecies had come true in Horace Pippin.

He invited Pippin to visit his famous collection of modern art in Merion, Pennsylvania. Pippin did so, but he was not overly impressed. He also accepted an invitation for him to attend the Barnes Foundation art school. But after attending a few classes, he left. He didn't think art could be taught. He said, "My opinion of art is that a man should have a love for it, because my idea is that he

David H. H. Felix, Philadelphia

Roses with Red Chair is how Horace Pippin titled this painting. It is characteristic of a number of paintings he made of flowers, usually in a vase set upon a doily which Pippin traced out elaborately. He considered his paintings to be very realistic.

paints from his heart and mind. To me it seems impossible for another to teach one of art."

In New York, Pippin's work was shown at the Downtown Gallery, a pioneer show place of modern art, in one of the largest shows of the work of Black artists ever assembled in that period. He was given major shows in Chicago at the Arts Club, at the San Francisco Museum of Art and the Carnegie Institute Museum of Fine Art in Pittsburgh. Yet he remained an isolated and lonely artist. West Chester was a small town. Other Black artists were delighted to see the recognition accorded him, but none really knew him. While Pippin met some of them, it was usually only at exhibitions of his work, after which he went quietly back to West Chester.

Like many other Black artists, Pippin was attracted by the life of abolitionist John Brown. Pippin's grandmother had told him many times of having been present when John Brown was hanged after his attempt to start an insurrection among the slaves of the South. This led Pippin to paint a series of three paintings of John Brown— reading his Bible, on trial, and on his way to be hanged. In *John Brown Going to His Hanging*, nearly all the spectators face the wagon in which John Brown is being taken to the gallows. In the foreground, looking at the viewer with a face that is both sad and angry, is a Black woman. She has turned her back on the hanging of John Brown. Many people believe that she represents both Pippin's grandmother and Black people in general.

With World War II now in full fury, Pippin yearned more than ever for an end to strife and turmoil. He had always consoled himself by reading his Bible. Occasionally he painted scenes from its stories as he imagined them. He now began a painting which he called *The Holy Mountain*. It represented his hope for peace among all men.

In his painting he showed all kinds of animals which are considered natural enemies lying side by side in peace.

His friends wanted to know what the painting meant. He wrote about it this way:

> To my dear friends: To tell you why I painted the picture. It is the holy mountain, my Holy Mountain.
> Now my dear friends,
> The world is in a bad way at this time. I mean war. And men have never loved one another. There is trouble every place you go today. Then one thinks of peace. . . .

Mrs. Galen Van Meter, Southport, Connecticut

The Holy Mountain I was the first of a series of paintings by Pippin near the end of his life. Based on the Bible, all of the paintings show basically the same scene—man and all the animals of the world at peace.

He mentions how reading Isaiah 11:6–10, inspired his painting:

> To think that all the animals that kill the weak ones will dwell together, like the wolf will dwell with the lamb, and the leopard shall lie down with the kid and the calf and the young lion. . . .
>
> Now my picture would not be complete of today if the little ghost-like memory did not appear in the left of the picture.
>
> As men are dying, today the little crosses tell us of them in the first World War and what is doing in the South to-day—all of that we are going through now. But there will be peace.

Pippin made four versions of *The Holy Mountain*. He was working on the last of them when, on July 6, 1946, he died of a stroke. Two weeks later his wife died.

Pippin's career as a recognized painter had lasted barely ten years. Yet in that short period, with a genius that overcame the handicap of his war-shattered arm, without training or even much general education, Horace Pippin established himself as a master of color and design. His is one of the most spectacular careers in American art.

AUGUSTA SAVAGE
(1900–1962)

This small statue, *Pugilist*, reflects Augusta Savage's great skill at characterization. Unfortunately, because she could not afford to have work cast in bronze, many of her statues have been damaged or destroyed.

One day, about 1906, a six-year-old Black girl was playing with some of the red clay that was found everywhere in Green Cove Springs in northern Florida. The town was famous for its bricks. But this little girl made a discovery. She found that you could roll that sticky clay into a kind of oval, give one end of it a pointy upswing, squeeze another piece into a long neck and stick it on—and you had made a duck. And she discovered that if she tried harder, she could make it look like a real duck—with its neck gracefully curved and head tucked down or stuck straight out with wings spread as though it was trying to take to the air or lurching in an awkward waddle on a foot made from a twig. Or a mother duck—being followed by a string of baby ducks.

She was delighted with what she could do. She showed her playmates and her brothers and sisters how to do it.

Although she did not know it then, she had started something she could not stop: artistic creation with her hands, in clay, in stone, sometimes in wood. Shaping things with her strong hands was an act that was deeply fascinating and satisfying to her. It was like a hunger that could not be appeased. Later, when as Augusta Savage she was known as an outstanding sculptor, she often thought about the little ducks. "They are a mystery," she said. "We didn't own any ducks. What did I see in ducks? Why ducks? Why start with ducks? Yet I did." She never found the answer.

But her impulse to create them developed into a young Black woman's difficult struggle for artistic expression that is unique. Because she was very poor, because she was Black, because she was a woman, her path was exceedingly harsh and rocky. Her struggles, often bitter, made her dedicated and demanding—of herself and of others. People spoke of her as "difficult" for she spared no one—especially not herself. Yet in her determined drive to succeed as an artist, she was like a stone cast in a pond. Her struggle changed many things for Black artists.

Augusta was the seventh child born to a struggling Methodist minister and his wife. They were very poor. Seven more children came after her, but of the fourteen, only nine lived to adulthood.

Life for the whole family was hard. Her father was strict and stern. Toys and playthings were practically unknown—which may have been why Augusta needed to make ducks. In such a large family, with so many voices trying to be heard, Augusta learned to speak up. She attended a school for Black children that had few books. Bright and alert, she learned rapidly, but the teacher could not give any one pupil much attention. Soon Augusta was playing hooky—going to the clay pits to model ducks, animals, human figures.

The family of poet James Weldon Johnson, who later became famous for his poems and songs and as a leader in the National Association for the Advancement of Colored People, lived in fairly comfortable circumstances in nearby Jacksonville. According to his autobiography, his family was close, happy, creative, and loving. But the family of Augusta was too poor to be very happy and its members were often frustrated and angry. Her father, a man who loved good books but could not afford them, was very upset to find that she was playing hooky and slipping off to make ducks and figures. An extremely religious and strict man, he was anxious over her behavior. He feared that she was making "graven images." Years later, when she was a famous sculptor, she said that she had to hide anything she made of clay because it so upset her father. "My father licked me five or six times a week and almost whipped all the art out of me."

Sometimes everything seemed against her. On days when it rained, she watched the rain melt her clay ducks and chickens. They simply oozed away. Yet she persisted.

When she was fifteen years old, her father was transferred to a church in West Palm Beach. She could find no clay there. The family circumstances improved. The school was much better. She stopped playing hooky and got to know her teachers. The principal, Professor Mickens, took an interest in this lively, bright youngster. One day, riding with him on the school wagon as he moved some material to another school, Augusta saw a small factory, the Chase Pottery. Instantly her almost forgotten satisfaction in modeling clay overcame her. She leaped from the wagon and disappeared into the pottery. There she was found by Professor Mickens a few moments later. She was begging for clay from Mr. Chase, who was both startled and amused by this youngster pleading: "Please, please, give me some clay. I want to make something."

"What can you make? Are you a potter?"

"No, no, I want to make ducks, chickens, animals, people. Statues."

Mr. Chase scratched his head. He had worked with clay all his life, making everything from pots to vases and cemetery urns—not ducks, chickens or statues. Finally, with Professor Mickens' urging, he laughed and said, "All right. Get that bucket over there and fill it. That'll give you about twenty-five pounds of good clay.

With Professor Mickens' wagon, she got the clay home and set to work. Her father, reassured by Professor Mickens, watched her excited work begin. The more she worked, the calmer she became. The next day she called her father to see what she had made—an eighteen-inch statue of the Virgin Mary. Her father was moved by the religious feeling expressed in her statue. He regretted the harshness he had shown earlier.

Professor Mickens then surprised Augusta. He insisted that she begin teaching, as part of the public school art program, a class in clay modeling. He convinced Mr. Chase to donate the clay. And he got the school board to agree to pay Augusta, still a student herself, a dollar a day for every day she taught, for six months.

Thus, while she was still in high school, just as she shaped clay, Augusta was herself shaped toward an interest and a career in teaching. This eventually led to her enrolling at the Tallahassee Normal School, which developed teachers for the public schools; it is now Florida A&M College, famous for its football teams and great marching bands.

Eventually she dropped out because she wanted to learn about art—not Latin. Yet her interest in teaching remained and ultimately it became important in her life.

Augusta wanted only to be an artist. She had seen that the principal business of Palm Beach and West Palm Beach was catering to wealthy Yankees who had come to Florida to escape the cold northern winters. Why couldn't she make something to sell to them?

She knew that the Palm Beach County Fair, a major tourist attraction, was coming. One morning in 1919 she appeared at the office of the superintendent of the fair, George Graham Currie. From a basket she placed before him a charming array of ducks, chickens, and other animals. "I want to sell these at the fair. Can I have permission for a booth?"

George Currie, an unusual and sensitive man who wrote poetry in his spare time, was fascinated by this talented girl and her clay ducks. He granted her permission, advising her only to "make some for every pocketbook."

Her prices ranged from 25¢ to $5. The county fair officials had been upset when George Currie gave permission to a Black girl to have a booth. Now they were delighted to hear tourists praising her work and the fair as the "best ever." Mr. Currie got them to vote her a ribbon and a special prize of $25 for the most original exhibit. When the fair ended, Augusta had earned $175.

No one was more pleased than George Currie. He had

believed in her ability, and now he encouraged her to go to New York to become an artist. There he had once met Solon Borglum, a leading sculptor and the older brother of Gutzon Borglum, who later carved the heads of Washington, Jefferson, Lincoln and Theodore Roosevelt on the face of Mount Rushmore in the Black Hills of South Dakota. "I'll write him a letter telling him how good you are and ask him to help you," he promised.

Augusta thought that she might make more money by doing clay portraits of well-to-do Black people in Jacksonville. George Currie had her make his portrait. He mentions it in a poem he dedicated to her in his book, *Songs of Florida.*

Augusta went to Jacksonville. To her dismay, she found no one who wanted portraits made, particularly by an unknown girl. People asked: "Where have you studied? What prizes have you won? Is your work in museums? Have you any portraits to show? What do critics say of your work?"

To these questions, she had no answers. She was, she realized, caught in the vicious circle of all beginners who can't get work because they have no experience. But she was determined to break out of it. In the fall of 1920 she asked George Currie to write to Solon Borglum and she took the train to New York, arriving there with $4.60.

She went instantly to see Borglum. The famous sculptor kindly asked why she thought she could be a sculptor. She told him her life story.

"Young lady, I have been pleased to hear your story," he said, "but from what you say you have no money. The young ladies who come here to study with me are the children of the rich and pay immense fees."

He paused. "However, there is a very fine art school here in New York which charges no tuition. You should apply there. In fact I will send a letter to Miss Kate Reynolds who is the registrar there. If she can't get you in, come back to me." The school was Cooper Union.

At Cooper Union Augusta found that there were 142 names on the waiting list ahead of hers. But a young Black man, learning her plight, spoke up for her. He got Miss Reynolds to agree to see her work. Augusta had none. But a few days later, supplied with funds from friends and family, she was able to show Miss Reynolds the head of a Harlem minister. Meanwhile Borglum's letter had arrived. Miss Reynolds admitted Augusta.

That was October 1921. The sculpture course was a four-year program. Augusta was passed through the first year's course in one week, through the second year's course in a month. She was put into a life class under George T. Brewster, a sculptor who did portraits of many outstanding people. He had been a leading instructor at Cooper Union for twenty years.

But in February 1922, four months after she had begun, Augusta had to go to Miss Reynolds. "I have to stop school," she said sadly. "I have no more money. I have to get a job, otherwise I will be put out of my room."

Miss Reynolds, who had come to feel a great sympathy and admiration for this slender young student and her determination to become an artist, almost wept. She recognized that the prejudices against women as well as those against Black people were crushing Augusta. Miss Reynolds told Augusta not to give up. Through a friend she immediately got Augusta a temporary job. Then she called a meeting of the advisory council of Cooper Union.

To its members Miss Reynolds put a blunt question. Where they going to permit this talented Black student, one of the first of her sex to study sculpture at Cooper Union, to be cast aside because she had no money?

The advisory council of the tuition-free school had never had this question put before it. Free tuition had been in itself a big contribution. Could it also finance a student who otherwise couldn't support herself? Augusta's record at the school testified to her talent. Also there was the backing of her instructor, George Brewster. Having been trained at the Rhode Island School of Design in Providence, he knew the work of Edward M. Bannister, the Black artist of that city who had been a founder of the Providence Art Society and had won the bronze medal at the Philadelphia Centennial Exposition in 1876. He added his voice to Miss Reynold's recommendation that they supply financial aid to Augusta Savage.

With that, the council voted to support a student for the first time in the school's history. Augusta, summoned from her job, wept when she learned from Miss Reynolds that the school would finance her room, board, and carfare. She lived in a cheap room in Upper Harlem.

Meanwhile, others had learned of her difficulties. At the 135th Street branch of the New York Public Library, where Augusta went to read about African art of the past, Mrs. Sadie Peterson, a librarian, heard of her struggles to continue studying. She arranged for Augusta to make a portrait of Dr. W. E. B. Du Bois, commissioned by friends of the library. It is one of the finest busts of him ever made. Soon others were arranging commissions for busts of other prominent Black leaders. One was for a portrait of Marcus Garvey, then at the height of his fame as the leader of the United Negro Improvement Association program, which was awakening America's Black people to take pride in their African heritage. These commissions not only helped her financially, but they gave her a certain recognition within the Black community. Moreover, she gained from them a sense of the need for

Black leadership and the human qualities required for it. While Dr. Du Bois and Marcus Garvey were political opposites, both were concerned with redefining relationships between white men and Black men. This became something that increasingly absorbed the energy and interest of Augusta Savage.

Augusta stayed in George Brewster's classes for three years, long after she was making portraits of prominent Black leaders. She supported herself with odd jobs—clerking, work in laundries, ironing. She had gradually come to realize that Brewster's portraiture was at best academic and at times pretentious. Years later, when she had gained some perspective on her talent, she summed her feelings up in a terse phrase: "I didn't know how good I was."

Mrs. Amy Jacques Garvey and Quito O'Brien Studios, Jamaica, B.W.I.

Mrs. Amy Jacques Garvey, widow of Marcus Garvey, posed with this bust of the great Black nationalist by Augusta Savage. Mrs. Garvey recalls that he sat for Miss Savage on Sunday mornings in their Harlem apartment.

In 1922 she learned that the French government was going to open a summer art school at the Palace of Fontainebleau outside Paris. It announced that 100 American women students would be admitted, their selection to be determined by a committee of eminent American artists and architects. Tuition would be free, but each young lady would have to supply her fare to France and living expenses. This would amount to $500.

Augusta decided she wanted to go. She won the approval and financial support of friends, quickly obtained pledges for the needed $500 and paid a $35 application fee.

She was informed by the committee that she had to supply two recommendations. But before she could forward them, her $35 was returned and she was told that the committee "with regret" had not approved her application.

Augusta was badly hurt. She wept with disappointment and rage in her room at 228 West 138th Street. For she knew she was more qualified than some students who had been accepted. She quietly returned to her Black friends the money they had given her. In a certain sense, there was nothing new in this kind of rejection. All Blacks had experienced it.

What was new was that a group of eminent artists, who are traditionally freer of racial prejudice than most groups, should behave this way, and in spite of the fact that the contributions of Black soldiers in World War I and mass demonstrations against the lynchings had made most educated Americans aware of the injustices under which America's Black citizens were laboring. With the same kind of courage that had brought her to New York in the first place, Augusta decided to fight.

One night a few weeks later, Alfred W. Martin, a leader of the Ethical Culture Society of New York, was lecturing in a Harlem branch of the New York Public Library.

After the lecture he was told what had happened to Augusta. Shocked, he promised to investigate. He wrote Ernest Peixotto, the internationally famous artist who had headed the committee, and asked if Augusta Savage had been excluded because of her race. Peixotto wrote back that she had been excluded because her application had not been properly accompanied by two recommendations, but then he went on "frankly" to state that the committee had felt this avoided a situation that would have been difficult for many Southern students who were being accepted. Since they would have to travel on the same ship and study in the same classes, this would also have been "embarrassing" to Miss Savage, said Peixotto.

With that the storm broke. Mr. Martin called the New York newspapers and denounced Miss Savage's exclusion as flagrant racial discrimination. He urged the committee, which included among others Edwin H. Blashfield, president of the National Academy of Design, James Gamble Rogers, representing the Society of Beaux Arts Architects, and Hermon A. MacNeil, a sculptor who had headed the National Sculpture Society, to reconsider.

Augusta Savage, then only twenty-three, found herself besieged by New York newspaper men. Coolly but impressively, she told her story. "I don't care much for myself," she said, "because I will get along all right here, but other and better colored students might wish to apply sometime. This is the first year the school is open and I am the first colored girl to apply. I don't like to see them establish a precedent." She added, "Democracy is a strange thing. My brother was good enough to be accepted in one of the regiments that saw service in France during the war, but it seems his sister is not good enough to be a guest of the country for which he fought."

Front-page stories continued day after day. Harlem

ministers and eminent educators, like the Columbia University anthropologist Dr. Franz Boas, assailed the committee. Alfred W. Martin sailed to France to protest in person to the French government. Dr. Emmett J. Scott of Howard University compared it to a recent lynching in Missouri. The *Nation* magazine and leading newspapers joined the protest. Dr. Boas in a public letter to Ernest Peixotto, said: "I cannot understand how the Committee could be willing to expose itself to the ridicule of all Europeans by taking a stand dictated by narrow racial prejudice." Peixotto sailed to France to try to explain the committee's action and nullify the protest now urging the French government to intervene.

Augusta herself wrote a long thoughtful letter to the New York *World* published on May 20, 1923. In it, she said in part: "One of the reasons why more of my people do not go in for higher education is that as soon as one of us gets his head up above the crowd, there are millions of feet ready and waiting to step on that head and crush it back again to dead level of the commonplace, thus creating a racial deadline of culture in our Republic. For how am I to compete with other American artists if I am not to be given the same opportunity?

"I haven't the slightest desire to force any questions like that of 'social equality' upon anyone. Instead of desiring to force my society upon 99 white girls, I should be pleased to go over to France in a ship with a black captain, a black crew and myself as sole passenger if on my arrival there, I would be given the same opportunity for study as the other 99 girls; and I feel sure that my race would not need to be ashamed of me after the final examination."

The committee hid in silence. One of its members was now bitterly ashamed of having participated in its decision. He was Hermon MacNeil, famous for his sculptures of American Indians. In Paris he had once shared a studio with Henry Ossawa Tanner and considered himself a friend of Tanner's. In the fashion of many white liberals, he had gone along with the committee, thinking it would spare Augusta Savage humiliation. He hadn't recognized his own acceptance of racial prejudice. Now he realized his mistake. He tried to get the committee to change its views. When that failed, he apologetically tried to make amends by asking Augusta Savage to come and work with him in his studio on College Point. She accepted.

But something else had happened. Augusta Savage had become the youngest nationally known sculptor. She had dramatically demonstrated the way in which well-educated Americans practiced and accepted racial discrimination. Among Black people she was recognized not only as an artist but also as a leader. And she made many Black people aware for the first time that they had among them fine artists and sculptors.

At the same time she was feared and hated by many prominent critics, museum heads, artists, and art dealers whose racial prejudice she had exposed. "She's got talent but she's a troublemaker. Look out for her," they said. No one knows how many times she was excluded from exhibits, galleries, and museums on this score.

Unable to sustain herself by her art, Augusta worked in factories and in laundries. When she could, she continued her efforts as a sculptor, carving in wood at times but usually modeling in clay. However, she was not forgotten by Dr. Du Bois, who was always urging support of young Black artists, in the pages of *Crisis*. In 1926, she showed her work at the Sesquicentennial Exposition in Philadelphia. That year Dr. Du Bois secured a scholarship for Augusta at the Royal Academy of Fine Arts in Rome.

It provided not only tuition, but also working materials, which is a financially heavy burden for sculptors. But it did not provide travel or living expenses.

Rome had been the world center of sculpture for centuries. Augusta wanted desperately to go. But she had no money. Appeals made on her behalf by friends fell on deaf ears. Although she had been able to raise pledges of $500 three years before, she was not now able to raise the $1,500 that was needed to take her to Rome and maintain her there.

Once again, Augusta suffered a hard blow. She saw that the Black artist was trapped in the economic plight of the Black people as a whole. Only the white middle-class seemed generally able to afford the luxury of allowing its gifted children to develop as artists. But she was sustained by her own determination, by the knowledge that Henry Ossawa Tanner had managed to win major prizes in Paris and that another Black woman sculptor, Meta Vaux Warrick Fuller, had studied at the Colarossi Academy in 1899 and later with Rodin. Such knowledge was psychologically sustaining as she sweated and toiled in steaming Manhattan laundries.

When she could, she kept working at her sculpture, modeling small figures, making portraits of ordinary people, occasionally getting a commission. She created a head of Theodore Upshure, a handicapped Greenwich Village Black youth, which impressed many artists. From time to time she exhibited her work at the 135th Street branch of the New York Public Library. She also sent some of it to Baltimore to be shown in the Frederick Douglass High School. In her studio at 29 West 130th Street in March 1927, she showed a small statue she called *The New Negro*, inspired by the anthology of that title edited by Dr. Alain Locke.

One day on a Harlem street she encountered an attractive young boy and coaxed him into posing for her. Soon she had created a head in clay that caught the vitality, the humanity, the tenderness, and the wisdom of a boy child who has lived in the streets. She scratched the title *Gamin* into its base.

Not long after it was created, it was seen by Eugene Kinckle Jones of the National Urban League and John E. Nail, a prominent Harlem real estate man. They agreed that something had to be done to give Augusta an opportunity to develop under the best artists in Europe.

Mr. Jones presented a plea on her behalf to the Julius Rosenwald Fund, which had been established by the chairman of the board of Sears, Roebuck & Company to help minority groups; it had given aid to many Black scholars and schools for Black children in the south. An art expert was assigned by the fund to examine Augusta's work. His enthusiasm brought Augusta two successive Rosenwald Fund fellowships. In addition, the usual fellowship of $1,500 was increased to $1,800 per year.

When it was announced that Augusta was at last to get the opportunity to study in Europe, many Black people came forward to help pay for her travel and wardrobe expenses. So that her Rosenwald scholarship might be spent entirely on study and art materials, fund-raising parties were held in Harlem. Many women's groups contributed. Black teachers at Florida A&M College in Tallahassee, where Augusta had been a student briefly, sent $50. Artists held receptions for her in Harlem and in Greenwich Village.

Soon Augusta was in Paris, studying portrait sculpture at the Grand Chaumière, one of its most modern art schools, under Félix Beuneteaux, twice winner of the Grand Prix of Rome. "Although he does not speak Eng-

Schomburg Collection, New York Public Library

Gamin, Augusta Savage's most popular statue, was modeled from the head of a real Harlem boy. It immediately won for her a fellowship to study in Europe. In 1967 it attracted great crowds at City University of New York when shown with the work of 250 other Black artists.

lish, we manage to understand each other," she wrote Eugene Kinckle Jones. "He is very strict but patient with me. I am very sure that I shall be able to make great progress under his instruction. He promises to enter my work in the Salon in May, if I work hard."

Her work was shown in European salons. She won an additional grant from the Carnegie Foundation to prolong her studies and spent months traveling through France, Belgium, and Germany, studying the sculpture of each country in their many cathedrals. She also studied with Charles Despiau, one of the foremost modern portrait sculptors.

In exhibitions abroad Augusta won citations from the Salon d'Automne and the Salon Printemps de Grande-Palais in Paris. An African figure was chosen for a medallion at the French government's Colonial Exposition.

In her studies Augusta concentrated on learning the most modern technical skills. But even as she studied, she began to realize that she might never have use for them. The economic depression that followed the collapse of the New York Stock Market in 1929 was spreading around the world. She knew that when a painter of the stature of Henry Ossawa Tanner could not sell his work, there could be little demand for her sculpture.

On her return to the United States, she again turned to portraiture, creating busts of James Weldon Johnson and the renowned surgeon Dr. Walter Gray Crump, who did so much to help Black medical students. She also made many striking figure statues. She exhibited, along with other leading American artists, such as Max Weber, Robert Laurent, and Reginald Marsh, at the salons of America at the Anderson Art Galleries in New York. A statue she titled *Envy* attracted critical attention as did a head called *Martyr* and a black Belgian marble head, *A Woman of*

Martinique. She was the first Black woman elected to the National Association of Women Painters and Sculptors.

In her work Augusta Savage exhibited a sophisticated technical virtuosity. Some of her fellow Black artists were annoyed with this development. They considered, as James A. Porter of Howard University, put it, that she had "set aside her own convictions to learn techniques and to carve subjects that convey a certain joy of life—but which happen to be trivial."

While this may seem a harsh judgment, there is a certain truth in it. Yet, something profoundly more important was happening with Augusta Savage. The Depression, which had put more than twelve million Americans out of work and hit Black families hardest of all, was to change abruptly the direction of her work. Augusta saw that the opportunity of creating the kind of sculpture she had once dreamed of was gone, probably forever, for her.

While she did not abandon working, she turned her main energies toward finding and developing of young Black artists. She was making her living by teaching a small class in her studio on West 143rd Street. She went to the Carnegie Foundation and won a grant of $1,500 so that she could teach children too. This enabled her to find larger quarters at 239 West 135th Street, a basement which she soon turned into a mecca of creative activity. If a young boy or girl stopped in front of it to see what was happening, Augusta cried, "Come on in."

She took in talented youngsters, like young Robert Jones, who had won a Fisher Bodies model contest in Virginia, had brought his model to New York, and then, without money, had had to sleep in parks. She found ways to feed and house him and brought him into her class. She attracted the gifted children in Harlem like a magnet. One of those who came into her circle was a youngster who had spent most of his time searching in Harlem for a way in which he could express his creativity. His name was Norman Lewis. Augusta taught him drawing and got him started in painting. Eventually she was to see him acknowledged as one of America's leading modern painters; his work was shown in major museums and he won a prize at the Carnegie International Exhibition in Pittsburgh in 1955.

She poured out warmth and enthusiasm. William Artis, a lonely orphan, also became a gifted artist under her tutelage. So did Ernest Crichlow, who traveled from Brooklyn to Harlem to attend her classes. What astonished and delighted these young artists was that this talented woman artist, whose name was known throughout Harlem for her work, who had studied in Europe, had come back to Harlem and was freely available to them. The fact that she had come back from Europe to settle in Harlem—to throw her classes and studio open to anyone who would come in to work at painting, drawing or carving—impressed all Harlem. Soon she had some sixty students working in her studios.

There was another aspect to her activities at this time. When the Depression worsened and it became plain that jobs, not relief, were desperately needed, Augusta took a leading role in helping to establish the right of Black artists to be enrolled on the Works Progress Administration art project. This federal project provided jobs for artists who worked at easels, as well as mural painters and sculptors.

The white administrators of the WPA art project at first were reluctant to believe there were Black artists. The files of the Harmon Foundation exhibits, kept by Mary Beatty Brady, immediately established the existence of nearly 200 artists who had exhibited, many of whom had won prizes. There were artists in Chicago, in San Francisco, in the Black universities and colleges. Many artists such as James A. Porter at Howard University, Hale Woodruff, then at Talladega College in Alabama, Archibald Motley, Jr., Joseph Delaney, Jesse C. Stubbs, Alan Rohan Crite, Samuel Joseph Brown, Elton Clay Fax, and many others participated in this struggle to secure recognition for Blacks as artists. White art educators, critics and artists who had never heard of Black artists were astonished.

In this struggle Augusta Savage became one of the most effective spokesmen and leaders of the Black artists. Ten years earlier the struggle over her rejection for Fontainebleau had given her a fierce conviction, unshakable determination, and the knowledge of how to tear the lies of racism apart. She knew how to deal with the press, to arouse support, to pressure politicians. Government bureaucrats were left speechless when she led delegations to demand recognition of Black artists, to demand that Black artists be given assignment to paint murals in hospitals, schools, libraries, and post offices.

In order to develop among Black artists an awareness of the issues and a solidarity in their struggles—political, social, artistic—she organized a club called The Vanguard, which met weekly at her studio. This led to her being attacked as a Communist, which she was not. But this did not deter her from attempting to win for every Black man, woman, and child the right to full participation in everything America offered. Conservative art circles warmed over tales of her being a wel-known "troublemaker," distorting the story of Fontainebleau.

One of her goals was to win the right of Black artists of superior training and ability to be supervisors in the WPA art projects, including their right to supervise white artists. Augusta Savage was one of the principal organizers of the Harlem Artists Guild. Aaron Douglas, whose murals and book illustrations had won him national recognition, was its first president. Augusta Savage was elected its next president—an indication of the esteem in which she was held by her fellow artists in Harlem.

"Augusta had a way with people," say most of the Harlem artists today. She could cajole, she could laugh, she could coax, but what most of them remember too was that she could be sharp, demanding, capable of being imperious and angry if she was not taken seriously. By the mid-thirties she was in charge of one of the largest art centers in the federal arts programs, the Harlem Community Art Center. The program, which she had organized with divisions for recreation and education as well as for serious art study, had some 1,500 Harlem residents enrolled.

Practically all her time and energy went into these organizational and educational efforts. Although she continued to create serious studies, such as *Realization*, a work which was cast in bronze through contributions from many Harlem citizens, her work was increasingly humorous. Her two small dancing figures, *Suzi-Q* and *Truckin'*, are examples. It was this type of work that prompted Porter and others to call her work "frivolous."

Yet the young artists extended themselves to win her praise, her thoughtful and often sharp attention. She would stand for no foolishness. She impressed them all with the idea that only through hard work and sacrifice could they succeed as artists.

When friends pointed out that she was spending her energies on political struggles and teaching, Augusta Savage told them what she really thought in a sharp self-assessment. "I have created nothing really beautiful, really lasting," she said. "But if I can inspire one of these youngsters to develop the talent I know they possess, then my monu-

At work in her studio, Augusta Savage preferred to model with clay rather than to carve. Believing profoundly in the talent of Black youngsters, she drew them into her studio and warmly encouraged them.

Hansel Miethe, *Life,* Copyright © Time, Inc.

ment will be in their work. No one could ask more than that."

Her last major work was a commission for the 1939–40 New York World's Fair. She took for her inspiration the great song, "Lift Every Voice," written by fellow Floridians Rosamond and James Weldon Johnson. She modeled a vast harp, sixteen feet tall, whose strings tapered down from the heads of a line of singing Black boys and girls. The base of the harp was formed by a mammoth forearm and hand with the fingers curving gently upward to complete the support. Kneeling in front of this representation of musical gifts of the Black people, a Black youth tenders this gift to mankind through outflung arms.

The World's Fair provided no money for casting the statue in bronze. Instead it was cast in plaster, then finished in a semblance of black basalt. Thousands of pictures of it were spread throughout the world by the fair's publicity office, making it probably Augusta Savage's best known work, certainly the most widely seen. After the fair, because she had no money for casting it into metal or for storing it, her work was smashed by bulldozers as part of the fair's clean-up.

Shortly after World War II began, the WPA art project ended. A few years later Augusta saw one of her favorite protégés, Jacob Lawrence, win recognition as one of America's most gifted artists. Not long after, she gave up teaching and moved to a farm near the art colony at Woodstock, New York, in the Catskill Mountains. There she worked quietly from time to time. She had married Robert L. Poston some years before. When her health became poor, her daughter, Mrs. Irene Allen, induced her to come back to New York City. There she died on March 27, 1962.

In 1967 the Harlem Cultural Council, the New York Urban League, and the City University of New York joined together to stage the largest show of the work of Black artists ever held in this country. Approximately 250 works, showing the evolution of Afro-American artists from the colonial days down to artists active in 1950, were assembled in the Great Hall of the university. Some were former students of Augusta Savage and had collaborated with her on many struggles to win recognition for Black artists.

More than 250,000 people came to see this mammoth exhibit of works that ranged from Joshua Johnston's portraits to the religious paintings of Henry Ossawa Tanner to the most modern abstractions. However, the work that attracted the most attention, the most favorable comments, was *Gamin*, the head of a boy created by Augusta Savage. Now nearly fifty years old, this statue testifies to the uniqueness of an artist whose potential was never fully realized. Yet her energy, sympathy, and insight significantly altered the lives of a number of America's young Black artists who emerged during those crucial Depression years.

JACOB LAWRENCE
(1917–   )

In the North the Negro had better educational facilities is part of Lawrence's migration series.

When they moved from Philadelphia to Harlem, Mrs. Rosalee Lawrence was worried about her son Jacob. She was still at work when he came home from school. Although he was a quiet, serious boy, she was afraid that Jake, as everyone called him, would be drawn into a gang of wild boys in his search for new friends.

Nearly twelve years old, Jake was finding Harlem exciting. Everything seemed to happen on its streets. There were children playing games, lovers walking hand in hand, street preachers, families on the steps of old brownstones, checker-players on the curb, evictions, police arrests, hard-running packs of boys.

Jake had been born in Atlantic City, New Jersey, on September 7, 1917. His father was a cook on railroad dining cars. His job kept him moving from one city to another. The family lived in Atlantic City, then Easton, Pennsylvania, then Philadelphia. This constant moving about led the parents to separate. Finally, Mrs. Lawrence and Jake moved to New York because the big city had more jobs for Black people than anywhere else. The Depression, just beginning, had already hit Black people. Mrs. Lawrence barely managed to make ends meet.

She made up her mind to keep Jake "off the streets." One day she learned that the Utopia Children's Center, a settlement house, had an after-school program of arts and crafts for children, and she promptly enrolled Jake in it. "I found a nice place for you to go after school, Jake," she told him. "You can make things."

"What kind of things?" asked Jake.

"Better see for yourself," his mother said. Next day she took him there. Charles Alston, a thin young man later to become a leading Black artist himself, was in charge. He showed Jake that he could carve soap, work with carpentry tools, weave baskets, draw, or paint.

"Can I color with crayons?" asked Jake.

"Of course," said Charles. He gave Jake a large box of crayons. "Make what you like."

Jake thought about something he liked to see: the patterns in little rugs at home and how regular they were. Certain shapes appeared again and again in alternating colors, pleasant and reassuring in their regular rhythm.

Soon Jake was carefully drawing geometrical patterns— triangles, squares, circles. He crayoned each section with another color. He delighted in working out the shapes so that they intersected at the proper angle. Thus a square could be made into two triangles which could be divided

William Lane, Leominster, Mass.

Always alert to patterns, Jacob Lawrence was naturally attracted
to checkerboards. His players have a joyless intensity very different from the mood of the domino players that Pippin painted.

endlessly into more triangles. Circles could lie within circles and then be cut into fat or thin pieces of pie. By
alternating colors, a checkerboard pattern would appear.
Although his patterns often resembled those in the little
Persian-type rugs his mother had, the colors were his own
—bold, contrasting yet harmonizing. And Jake began to see
patterns all about him—the windows in buildings, people sitting around a table, the subway steps, the legs of
people walking together, fire escapes. All these formed
patterns and he enjoyed recognizing them.

Alston was impressed with Jake's serious concentration.

He was even more impressed with the fact that Jake didn't whine, "What should I do next, teacher?" Jake had ideas about what to do. His questions were about *how* to do something. Alston was completing his work for a master's degree in education at Columbia university's Teachers College. He decided that, as he said later, "It would be a mistake to try to teach Jake. He was teaching himself, finding his own way. All he needed was encouragement and technical information."

The streets of Harlem continued to fascinate Jake. One day he began painting street scenes inside cardboard boxes. He would cut away one side of a box and discard its top and bottom. Then on the inside of the three remaining sides he would draw and paint a neighborhood scene—the brownstone houses with clumps of people on the steps, bars with bright signs, furniture stores with giant bargain sale signs, tenement fire escapes, funeral parlors, the broken windows of an abandoned tenement, the barbershop, and the hole in the block left by a collapsed building. These three-sided boxes were like small models of stage sets. Yet Jake had never seen a stage set. What he had seen was the neighborhood—and he reproduced the way it looked and felt in a striking, three-dimensional way.

Among the center's magazines Jake found an article that showed how W. T. Benda, a famous artist, made masks of papier-mâché. Charles Alston showed Jake how to make papier-mâché by mixing paper pulp, water, and paste. Then Jake set about making masks like Benda's—fantastic gargoyles, animals, and birds, realistic faces with decorative headdresses, and caricatures that were more like Halloween masks. Sometimes he painted the masks. At other times, he colored them with delicate pastel chalks.

Watching him develop, Alston became convinced this serious lad was one of the most naturally gifted artists he had ever seen. He could not keep his delight in Jake's work a secret. He proudly showed it to his Harlem artist friends. All were impressed.

Soon many Harlem artists were encouraging young Jake Lawrence. All were having a hard time, working at part-time jobs, struggling to meet the rent, buy paint and canvas. But they recognized talent. Their unspoken fear was that a brilliant young talent like Jake Lawrence would be crushed in the oppressive poverty of Harlem as the Depression grew worse. None of these artists could offer Jake a job or protect him from harsh social and economic difficulties of the times. But they quietly sought him out on visits to Alston, told him they had seen and liked his work. They steadily brought him into their ranks and treated him with respect and warmth. Asking "How's the painting going, Jake?" they encouraged him even though, as they often joked, "There's no future in it."

Thus these Black artists were the first to recognize one of the most creative artists in America today.

By this time Jake had outgrown the after-school program. He was a high school teen-ager, hunting hungrily for odd jobs, for old bottles that could be returned to stores for pennies. The Depression had worsened. His mother had lost her job and gone on relief. Jake eased her problems by enrolling in the CCC, the Civilian Conservation Corps. Living out in the country, in barracks, the CCC boys planted trees, drained swamps, cleared dead trees from forests, and built flood-control dams. In an upstate New York camp, Jake learned many new things.

Still the Depression got worse and worse. Millions more lost their jobs. To provide jobs, President Franklin D. Roosevelt established the Works Progress Administration. Called the WPA, it put millions of unemployed to work building schools, hospitals, post offices, roads, and airports.

It set up theaters for actors, writing projects for writers, and art projects for artists such as making murals for hospitals, schools, and post offices. In Harlem the art project combined art, education, and recreation. Soon some 1,500 people were attending art sessions in Harlem.

For the first time many Black people learned that they had talented artists in their midst. Harlem Community Art Center was at 125th Street and Lenox Avenue. It was directed by the sculptor Augusta Savage. Another was set up in the basement of the 135th Street Public Library. Still another, headed by Charles Alston, operated at 306 West 141st Street. Alston and Henry "Mike" Bannarn, a sculptor, lived in the building at 141st Street. This became a major gathering place for Harlem artists, writers, modern dancers, intellectuals, and musicians. There they could exchange ideas, work together, help one another.

When Jake came back from the CCC, he painted at the center his first Harlem scenes, such as street preachers and sick people at the clinic.

One day, leaving the YMCA where he liked to shoot pool, Jake stopped at the door of a crowded meeting room. The speaker, a slender erect man, said Black people were never going to get anywhere until they knew their own history and took pride in it. Jake edged into the room. The speaker described the achievements of Black men in Africa, the golden city of Timbuktu, African use of iron when most of Europe was ignorant of it, the elegant bronze casting required to create the superb art treasures of Benin in Nigeria.

"Who's the man talking?" asked Jake.

"Don't you know? That's Professor Seyfert."

Jake soon found out that "professor" was an honorary title bestowed on Charles Christopher Seyfert by his friends and admirers. Originally a carpenter, he had collected in his home a sizable library on African cultures and the contributions of Black people to American life. Many Harlem people came regularly to listen to his talks on their history, a "black studies" program existing years before such programs were conceived by educators.

Professor Seyfert provided the intellectual break that young Jake Lawrence and other Harlem young people were looking for. It gave them a sense of dignity and pride and the feeling that they had something creative within themselves that could be developed. Jake had already found deep satisfaction in working as an artist. Soon he was absorbed in reading and studying Black history. The commercial high school he attended provided none of this satisfaction in its courses on bookkeeping.

Jake left school after his second year to devote himself to his new pursuits. This worried his mother. She had hoped that knowing bookkeeping would help Jake get a decent job. But Jake was excited by what he was learning from Professor Seyfert. He read avidly about anything or anyone that this unusual teacher mentioned—slave revolts, great African empires, black inventors, the Underground Railroad, Benjamin Banneker, Black soldiers in the American Revolution and the Civil War.

Professor Seyfert took a special interest in young Harlem artists. He believed that through their pictures they could show Black people their history and inspire them. He often invited Jake, Robert Pious, Earle Sweeting, and other artists to his home.

When, in 1935, the Museum of Modern Art exhibited sculpture from West Africa, Professor Seyfert rounded up groups of Harlem artists and took them there. He explained the origin and meaning of these unusual works. Jake missed going with a group and went alone. At the museum the solemn carved figures greatly excited him.

They were the work of Black men who totally disregarded the western white man's ideas, yet they were art. Jake studied them carefully. When he returned home, he got some blocks and made two small wooden sculptures. "I didn't have regular carving tools, so I whittled more than I carved," he recalled. "The show made a great impression on me." For weeks afterward the young Harlem artists talked of it.

Professor Seyfert's talks provided historical facts. But they also helped Jake feel he was part of the past struggles of Black people and their present struggles. He could pour his deep feelings into his paintings. His work was increasingly winning the praise of his fellow Harlem artists and he liked to visit Alston's and Bannarn's studio. There he might run into Aaron Douglas, Augusta Savage, Ronald Joseph, Robert Blackburn, Gwendolyn Bennett, Vertis Hayes, or Charles Sebree, or writers like Langston Hughes, Claude McKay, William Attaway, and Richard Wright. Younger artists like Norman Lewis and Romare Bearden were often there, as were composers Frank Gaskin Fields and Joshua Lee and dancer Ad Bates.

Yet Jake actually had less and less time to paint. He was too busy scurrying around trying to earn money. He delivered laundry, ran errands, worked for a small storefront printer who turned out handbills, business cards.

One day Augusta Savage learned from Jake that he hadn't been painting. Taking him by the arm, she headed down the street. "Where are we going?" asked Jake.

"To WPA headquarters! We're going to get you on the artists' project. You're an artist and you ought to be painting and getting paid for it. It's a shame!"

At WPA headquarters Jake's application was turned down. He was under twenty-one years of age. Jake just shrugged. He hadn't really believed he was going to get on the project. That would be just too much luck in a bad luck world. But Augusta was grim and sharp. "That's just one of their stupid rules," she said. "I'm going to get you on that project."

Jake forgot about it. By saving up his money, he bought a *Bronx Home News* delivery route. He gradually came to think of painting as something he would do as a hobby. And he was beginning to see that without an education, he was going to be permanently lined up for menial jobs. As one job played out, he found another. But one day, when he dropped into the Harlem Art Center, Augusta Savage said, "Come on, Jake. We're going to the WPA again. You're old enough now!"

She had kept track of Jake's birthday. A year had passed. It was July 1938 and he was now twenty-one. And this time he was accepted as an artist and assigned to the easel project. He could paint at home and was provided with materials and paid $23.86 a week. In return he had to deliver two paintings every six weeks.

Later, looking back, Jake said, "If Augusta Savage hadn't insisted on getting me on the project, I would never have become an artist. It was a real turning point for me."

During the eighteen months he was on the WPA project, Jake had time to develop his technique in working with water-based paints, which he preferred to oils. More importantly, it established him as an artist in his own mind and gave him confidence in the value of his work. And when he picked up his pay check at WPA headquarters, he met many other artists and writers, both Black and white. This gave him a broader perspective on all the arts. It also deepened his own interest in the area he knew best: the lives of Black people and their history.

Stimulated by Professor Seyfert, Jake had made extensive notes on the life of Toussaint L'Ouverture, who had led the Black people of Haiti in overthrowing slavery. He decided Toussaint L'Ouverture was a hero worth painting. When most artists want to show a famous historical character or event, they create a single painting—a triumphant entry, a general directing his troops or standing beside his cannon, surrounded by flags and advisers. But Jake felt there were so many important things he had to show about Toussaint L'Ouverture that he painted a remarkable series of forty-one paintings.

In his work Lawrence was not concerned with naturalistic details. The faces in his paintings often seem masklike. Yet the very stance and attitude of the characters leave no doubt as to their inner feelings and strength. In painting in this way Lawrence was concerned with the same kind of emotional reality that is seen in African sculpture. Lawrence likewise emphasized those aspects he considered important. Thus he often presented a scene—historic or contemporary—in its emotional truth.

His paintings were modern. While always recognizable, people and objects were presented in a flat, often angular, abstract way. He was sensitive to patterns emerging in his work, just as he had been when doing intense work with patterns as a boy. He often made patterns part of his composition, giving it greater dramatic strength than it would have had otherwise.

How Lawrence worked surprised even experienced artists. Instead of completing one painting in a series at a time, he penciled an outline drawing for each panel in the series. Then he mixed a color—say, a blue—and applied it to each section of each panel where he wanted it. Then he mixed the next color and applied it in the same fashion. Thus, he might be working on forty panels at once. The result was that the total series was completed with the last color. More important, the colors have a remarkable consistency

Division of Cultural Research, Department of Art, Fisk University, Nashville, Tenn.

No. 2 in his Toussaint L'Ouverture series was captioned by Lawrence as follows: *Mistreatment by the Spanish soldiers caused much trouble on the island and caused the death of Anacanca, a native queen, 1503. Columbus left soldiers in charge. Their greed for gold caused them to begin making slaves of the people who were living a happy and peaceful life up to that time. They naturally resisted. The queen was one of the leaders in the insurrection.*

throughout. But this method is also a demonstration of an unusual organizing and aesthetic ability, requiring a kind of planning few artists could achieve. And it, too, is derived from his pattern-making as a youngster, when he would put in all of one color in his design, then follow with the other colors one by one.

Lawrence's first formal show was held at the Harlem YMCA. When the WPA art project was closed, Alston and other artist friends helped him get a scholarship at the American Artists School where he studied with Anton

Refregier, Sol Wilson, and Eugene Morley. About that
time Lawrence received grants from the Rosenwald Fund
for three years running. These enabled him to continue.

About this time some leading New York art dealers,
stimulated by Dr. Alain Locke and Mary Beatty Brady of
the Harmon Foundation, had agreed to hold a large group
show of the works of Black artists. Then each gallery was
to select one artist and show his work regularly.

The show was assembled. It opened on December 8,
1941, the day after the Japanese attack on Pearl Harbor
pulled the United States into World War II. The artists'
work received good notices from the critics. But the con-
fusion of the war situation led all the dealers but one
to back down on their promises to select an artist to
represent. The exception was Edith Halpert of the Downtown Gallery, one of the leading art dealers in the nation
who selected unknown Jacob Lawrence.

Lawrence did not even see the show. At the Harlem
Art Center several years before, he had met a lovely girl
from the West Indies, a talented artist in her own right,
Gwendolyn Knight. By the time this show was prepared,
they had married and gone to New Orleans on a honey-
moon. This trip was actually part of his second Rosenwald
grant—to portray the great movement of the Black people
from the South to the cities and towns of the North.

Edith Halpert wrote Lawrence in New Orleans, asking
him to join her gallery. "It was one of the turning points
of my life," he said later. "I was on a fellowship and had
no idea of what I was going to do later. I had no idea of
going out and looking for a gallery to sell my work. I didn't
know the quality of gallery to look for. I didn't know
how artists turned professional. But I wrote back, 'Sure!
You can handle my work.' I had no idea that Edith Halpert
was one of the top dealers. It was really most fortunate

for me that I was selected by one of the top people in the business and that she became responsible for me."

Soon after this, Lawrence completed the series he called *The Migration of the Negro*. It portrayed in dramatic and moving terms the great northern migration of Black people between 1910 and 1940. Jake and Gwendolyn even went to the little Virginia village where his mother's folks had come from and made sketches.

These paintings were an enormous success. Word of them spread rapidly in New York art circles. Two leading museums, the Phillips Gallery of Washington, D.C., and the Museum of Modern Art in New York City, competed to buy the entire series when they were shown. At last the museums compromised, dividing the series between them. Art critics hailed the emergence of a new artist who had something to say. Few artists have ever made a more auspicious debut. Jake's mother, who had been terribly worried by his efforts to be an artist, was able to relax.

In 1943 Lawrence was inducted into the United States Coast Guard as a steward's mate, the only enlisted rating then open to Black men. He was assigned to the *Sea Cloud*, which carried the first racially mixed crew in the service. When, in St. Augustine, Florida, the crew members and their wives were invited to Christmas dinner, Jake and Gwendolyn showed up—and were snubbed. A white woman refused to sit next to Gwendolyn. Jake made some caustic drawings reflecting the situation, but later he called working aboard the *Sea Cloud* "the best democracy I've ever known."

Lawrence painted a series on Coast Guard life, which was first exhibited at the Museum of Modern Art in New York. Surrounded by beaming admirals, commanders, and other officers, Steward's Mate Lawrence was given special permission to attend. When the exhibit was moved to

A.   B.

C.   D.

Collection, The Museum of Modern Art. Gift of Mrs. David M. Levy

Learning of the great mass movement of Black people from the South during and after World War I, Lawrence painted a series, *The Migration of the Negro,* to show why. Two major museums wanted the series and finally shared it. One took the even numbered paintings, the other took the odd numbered ones. These are from New York's Museum of Modern Art.

A. *In every home people who had not gone North met and tried to decide if they should go North or not.*

B. *They were very poor.*

C. *Child labor and a lack of education was one of the other reasons for people wishing to leave their homes.*

D. *And the migrants kept coming.*

Boston and other cities, he accompanied it. His skipper, Lieutenant Commander Carleton Skinner, recognizing Lawrence's artistic talent, got him a public relations rating,

Specialist Third Class, so that he would have time to paint instead of working as a steward. With this new status, he was assigned to troopships, sailed to Italy and India. From his sketches he created a stark series called *War*.

After the war, he again returned to the history of Black people, aided by a Guggenheim Fellowship in 1946. He created a series on John Brown, another on Frederick Douglass, still another on Harriet Tubman. Paintings seemed to pour from him. He created series on the crafts and skills many Black people had developed, such as watch repairing, furniture making, and sewing, which gave a certain dignity to these crafts. In 1946 he also taught painting at Black Mountain College, an experimental school in North Carolina. In 1947 *Fortune* magazine sent him through the South to paint Black people in the new job and educational situations that industrialization was gradually creating there. He illustrated *One Way Ticket*, a book of poems by Langston Hughes.

More successful than he had ever dreamed, Lawrence now began to realize how difficult were the problems he was tackling. Like many other artists, he was extremely sensitive and filled with self-doubt about his own abilities. He had been, he felt, only lucky. His successes seemed unreal when so many of his friends were less well off. And this made him nervous and depressed.

Many artists have known such periods of emotional upheaval and depression. The famous Dutch artist Vincent Van Gogh is the best known example of such turmoil.

Fortunately Lawrence was able to talk with his wife Gwendolyn, also a painter, and with Dr. Emanuel Klein, both of whom gave him great help, reassurance, and understanding. He emerged from this period of despondency an even stronger person.

When his feelings of depression lifted, Lawrence worked

United Press International

While in the U. S. Coast Guard in World War II, Lawrence was
recognized as an important painter. His work was exhibited at
the Institute of Modern Art in Boston, which he is shown visiting.
He also had a show at the Museum of Modern Art in New York.

with greater skill than ever before. He created new paintings of Harlem scenes, sometimes amusing ones. In *Vaude-
ville*, he portrayed two slapstick clowns against a background filled with the kind of brilliant geometric patterns.

In the mid-1950s Lawrence created his monumental
series: *Struggle: From the History of the American People*.
He presented a pictorial history of America from the days
of the Indians down to the present day. Each panel demonstrated that what had been achieved had been won with
struggle. Under each painting he attached a documentary caption. For example, *Crossing the Delaware* bears

Courtesy of the Detroit Institute of Arts

John Brown formed an organization among the colored people of the Adirondack Woods to resist the capture of any fugitive slaves is how Lawrence titled this painting from his series on the life of John Brown. Again he approaches a subject that Horace Pippin treated in a very different manner.

this legend: "We crossed the river at McKonkey's Ferry 9 miles above Trenton . . . the night was excessively severe . . . which the men bore without the least murmur. . . .—Tench Tilghman, 27 December 1776."

This series of sixty paintings won for Lawrence his greatest acclaim. He poured everything he had learned about painting into them, creating subtle effects not present in earlier work. Once again the storytelling is emotionally moving and great incidents and personalities as well as the role of the common man are vividly portrayed.

Since then Lawrence has created another series in the form of a children's book on Harriet Tubman, called *Harriet and the Promised Land*. Because it is a book, it escapes the fate of many of his series—being broken up so that it is almost impossible to see the whole set. One exception to this division is the Toussaint L'Ouverture series. The Harmon Foundation gave Lawrence $100 as a loan against the series when he got married. He never redeemed it and the Harmon Foundation ultimately gave the series to Fisk University. It is often borrowed by other colleges and museums. Lawrence has been pleased with this. "If it hadn't been for the Harmon Foundation, the set would have been broken up, lost, and damaged. I am very happy that it is still intact and available," he says.

Lawrence was one of the first generation of artists who grew up in a Black urban community whose talent was recognized early by older Black artists and whose teachers were primarily Black artists. He therefore did not have some problems and conflicts faced by earlier generations.

He has always lived deep in the heart of a Black community, painting what he himself has seen and experienced and relating it to the past, with deep feeling and superb skill. Taken together, his paintings express in a powerful way, impressive in its intimate knowledge, the heroic struggles of the Black people in the New World.

In 1960 he was honored with a special retrospective show by the American Federation of Art, which produced a monograph on his work. In the mid-1960s he went to Africa, living and working primarily in Nigeria. For many years his paintings have been shown in Europe and Africa with acclaim. He taught for many years at the Art Students League of New York, one of America's best-known art schools, at Brandeis University, at the New School for Social Research, at California State College in Hayward. But he has taught longest at Pratt Institute, one of the nation's leading professional art schools. In 1970 Pratt appointed him professor of art and co-ordinator of arts, a distinguished appointment.

Recognition has also come to him from the National Institute of Arts and Letters which is composed of the nation's foremost writers, artists, and cultural leaders. In 1965 they elected him a member to honor his contributions to American life. At the same time Lawrence has continued to encourage the cultural achievements of his own people, helping to found the Black Academy of Arts and Letters in 1969.

In recent years, when the demand for a theory of "Black art" arose from some Black artists, Lawrence participated in many discussions of the subject. He pointed out that while the Black artist may be strongly motivated by his feeling of racial identity and seek to serve the cause of his oppressed people, "all this will be incidental in the final judgment of his work. It may be important for him to express himself but he's going to be judged by the criterion of the artists of all ages. And that judgment is not going to be on his motivation. That may be interesting to the historian and it may be interesting to just anyone, but it will have no validity when it comes to the question:

what contribution has he made in the plastic area of art? This is it.

"All artists have this problem, not only Negro artists. I think it can be more intensified for the Negro artists because of the general racial situation."

He called for massive government aid for all artists. "I think we must be careful not to isolate ourselves because many of the things we're talking about not only apply to the Negro artist but pertain to the artist generally. If they're accomplished by government art support, we will all benefit by them."

He continued: "I think the thing for us to pursue—and I repeat this—is not only to get massive aid and help within the Negro community, but also not to tear us away from the main community, not allowing people downtown to say, 'Well, let's give them a little something and we can forget about them.'"

Still young as painters go, Lawrence has many more contributions to make both as a teacher and as a leading American artist. In many ways he has only begun to paint.

Already he is a major influence for a number of young Black artists. One example is Vincent Smith who draws so much of his subject matter from the urban life of Brooklyn. And all of the younger Black artists acknowledge him as a contemporary pioneer in opening new doors for them. They include artists as diverse as printmaker Emma Amos; abstract colorist Betty Blayton; Floyd Coleman, who creates powerful social statements; leading sculptor Richard Hunt; William Majors, who creates large color field paintings and exquisite prints; and Raymond Saunders, whose wistful symbolic paintings are delicately defined.

It is small wonder then that in June 1970, meeting in Cincinnati where Robert S. Duncanson had made his great contributions to American painting, the National

Today one of America's best-known artists, Jacob Lawrence has taught in the nation's leading art schools. He began by making patterns and masks in a Harlem after-school center. Now his work hangs in museums nationwide.

Photo by Peter A. Juley & Son

Association for the Advancement of Colored People awarded Jacob Lawrence the Spingarn Medal, its highest award. Its citation hailed "his eminence among American painters" and paid tribute to his success in using "his artistic gifts and values to the portrayal of Negro life and history on the American scene" and to "the compelling power of his work, which has opened to the world beyond these shores, a window on the Negroes' condition in the United States." It concluded: "In salute to his unswerving commitment not only to his art, but to his black brother within the context of hope for a single society, the NAACP proudly awards this 55th Spingarn Medal to Jacob Lawrence, artist, teacher and humanitarian."

Jacob Lawrence is the first artist to be so honored.

And people are still responding, just as they did in the Utopia Children's Center so many years ago, to what he draws and paints.

INDEX